The Fourth Way

www.thefourthway.org.uk
A BOOK AND A MISSION

Also published in a handsome Russian-language edition by Book World, of St. Petersburg.

THE
FOURTH WAY
Guidelines for Tomorrow's World

Donald Wilhelm

SECOND EDITION

SHEPHEARD-WALWYN
LONDON
2000

© 1999 Donald Wilhelm

All rights reserved. No part of this book may be reproduced
in any form without written permission from the publisher,
Shepheard-Walwyn (Publishers) Ltd

First published in 1999 by
Shepheard-Walwyn (Publishers) Ltd
26 Charing Cross Road (Suite 34)
London WC2H 0DH

Second Edition 2000

British Library Cataloguing in Publication Data
A catalogue record of this book
is available from the British Library

ISBN 0 85683 178 6 cased
ISBN 0 85683 185 9 limp

Typeset by Rowland Phototypesetting Limited
Bury St Edmunds, Suffolk
Printed in Great Britain by
St Edmundsbury Press, Bury St Edmunds

To the Regeneration of Elegance

Contents

Acknowledgements ix
Preface xiii

I Vision and Blindness 1
II The Pragmatic Fixation 18
III Giants of Science 35
IV The Great Experiment 58
V Scientific Idealism 78
VI The Global Synthesis 99

Notes 125
Index 135

Acknowledgements

I am everlastingly indebted to my father – also Donald Wilhelm – who was a writer all his life and who taught me to write with allegedly reasonable lucidity. He was also one of the American Relief Administration team who went to the then Soviet Union at the time of the terrible famine following the Revolution. It was from him that I inherited my love of the Russian people, and he would be pleased that I am following in his footsteps. Likewise, I am deeply and permanently indebted to my devoted mother, who also worked for the American Red Cross.

For many fundamental insights I am enduringly grateful to Professor F. S. C. Northrop of Yale University and Professor Carl J. Friedrich of Harvard University. I am likewise indebted to a staggering number of other people too numerous to mention here. They will all know of my appreciation and they can realize that their thoughts have contributed to the synthesis.

I am deeply indebted to Anthony Werner, my British publisher, for his encouragement and for his valuable insights as the project developed. My wife Muriel (Renée) showed much patience and had many valuable suggestions. I extend my appreciation to Joanne Stevens for typing and checking the manuscript. Full responsibility for any errors of fact or interpretation of course rests with me alone.

This book owes much to the talent found in a beneficent

triangle of historic British cities including Cambridge, Bury St. Edmunds, and London. In Cambridge, my long-time friend Colin Walsh, of Book Production Consultants, gave very valuable strategic advice, and it was he who conceptualized what became the book's jacket/cover illustration. Dr. Peter Curtis-Prior of Cambridge has given particularly valuable overall judgements. Mitzi Godfrey has provided inspiration. Likewise I am indebted to Andrew R. Davidson, of the Cambridge firm First Edition Translations, for the design of the book and for the cover illustration by Vicky Slegg of The Write Idea and the index by Jackie Butterley.

My thanks go to Denis Harman of St. Edmundsbury Press, in Bury St. Edmunds, for the splendid and expeditious handling of the printing as well as for his unfailing sense of humour. Likewise I extend very warm appreciation to Kate Hawthorne and her London company known as Hatricks PR. She combines real competence with a wonderful musical and artistic background.

On the Russia side great credit goes to my dynamic friend Mr. Valery Agapitov, who is a real statesman of business. It was he who enunciated the fundamental principle that Russia's *economic* progress depends upon her evolving a new ideology. Likewise I am enormously grateful to Sergei V. Chistobaiev, the head of Book World, the lively St. Petersburg publishing house. In earlier years Russian books tended to look drab, but he has done a truly beautiful job with the Russian-language edition of this book. The book is being distributed all over that vast country with its eleven time zones.

Again it has been my privilege to have available a panel of Russian friends with pertinent insights and opinions. These include Natalie Alexandrova, Dr. Tatiiana Ianova, Dr. Igor Routchimski, Professor Dimitri Ruschin, Professor Vladimir Slivker, and Mariya Zobkova. Tatiana Niconorova, Natasha

Novokova, and Faina Borisovna Ozdoeva have given particularly perceptive comments on Russia's rich culture. My very special thanks must go to my skilled translator, Beltina Dianova, who has prepared the manuscript for the Russian-language edition of this book. She had already translated two of my previous books into Russian, and again with the new book she has shown her ability to convey the true spirit. In addition, she has helped me to understand the importance of that great Russian physicist Professor Alexander Popov (1859–1905), to whom I wish to pay special tribute.

Some men have a noble spirit, and that was certainly true of him. Popov and Guglielmo Marconi (1874–1937) were personal friends, and they – together with Heinrich Hertz (1821–1894), James Clerk Maxwell (1831–1879), and others – laid the theoretical foundations for what was to become a global radio communications network. In a scientific paper published in 1890, Popov clearly stated the following: "It is beyond question that the first practical results in wireless telegraphy over considerable distances have been attained by Marconi above all others." Marconi's work is further referred to in Chapter I of this book.

As a result of the communications revolution, modern man is bombarded by an ever-increasing volume of data which, unless he is very careful, can ruin his power to think. Today a lot of these data of course stream out over the Internet. But the Internet, if used with sufficient care and discrimination, can facilitate fresh thinking. That is the purpose of the website – www.thefourthway.org.uk – which accompanies this book.

DONALD WILHELM

Preface:

In the year 1998 a book was published which immediately became a sort of Bible for Britain's Prime Minister Tony Blair and America's President Bill Clinton and his wife Hillary. It was called *The Third Way: The Renewal of Social Democracy*. It was written by Anthony Giddens, an acknowledged guru of Mr. Blair, and it formed the basis for long-running Blair-Clinton discussions on the subject.

Yet in the words of *The Economist*, the internationally-respected London journal, "This book is awesomely, magisterially, and in some ways disturbingly vacuous." Two somewhat different assessments!

In the present volume it is part of my task to show that the so-called Third Way is in fact completely dated and obsolete. It represents merely the reappearance, under a flag of convenience, of the end-of-ideology syndrome of the 1960s. Far better options are available.

Much of our current intellectual confusion arises from over-specialization and over-compartmentalization, with the "expert" knowing more and more about less and less. The explosive growth of information technology or IT has merely compounded the problem.

It is much to the credit of Tony Blair and Bill Clinton that the Kosovo tragedy brought home to them the overriding importance of fundamental moral values. But they have had no adequate intellectual framework to accommodate those values. They, along with many of their contemporaries, have been stuck with a shallow and superficial ideology.

This present book exposes the superficiality of current Third Way thinking as well as the strengths and weaknesses of Karl Marx's famous Scientific Materialism. Drawing inspiration from the resounding success of the natural sciences, I delineate a new philosophy of Scientific Idealism. This is christened the Fourth Way, which can be described as much more solid and substantive than Third Way vagaries.

I approach this task with all humility. My work at Yale and Harvard, together with my overseas assignments in numerous countries, I hope equip me for the task.

Let me make an earnest request to the reader. To obtain a full and proper picture, the chapters should be read in strict sequence. In that way the argument will be seen to unfold systematically.

We can take an intellectual journey together in a spirit of exhilaration and adventure!

DONALD WILHELM

I Vision and Blindness

The world needs specialists. The world needs many kinds of specialists. With the advance of technology the world demands more and more specialists. They are indispensable to life in the developed world in the twentieth and twenty-first centuries. Yet at the same time one is reminded of the adage that the specialist is one who knows more and more about less and less until he knows everything about nothing.

The triumphant role of the specialist is well illustrated by the field of information technology or IT. Bill Gates became the world's richest man – even richer than the Sultan of Brunei – on the back of the IT revolution.[1] The computer and other information technology, in interaction with television technology, will more and more influence or dominate every aspect of our lives.

But the specialist's domination cannot go unchallenged. This becomes apparent when we consider the situation on the Planet Earth as its citizens entered the twenty-first century AD. Looking back, we can see that numerous countries had shown remarkable economic growth, and living standards had improved for millions of people. But at the same time people on the planet faced a depressing array of problems, most of which were of man's own making. They included malnutrition; overpopulation; unemployment and underemployment; physical and mental illness; educational and cultural deprivation; denial of civil liberties; soul-destroying work and leisure; separation and divorce; delinquency and crime; alcoholism and drug addiction; urban blight and sprawl; rural squalor; pollution and environmental deterioration; terrorism and insurrection; potential chemical, bacteriological and nuclear confrontation.

The specialist mentality has signally failed to tackle these and other problems decisively. Modern man has indeed developed a splendid ability to create such problems as the foregoing faster than he can solve them. We appear to be on a treadmill.

For a perspective-imparting contrast one can consider, for example, Edinburgh in Scotland some two centuries ago. By the second half of the eighteenth century Edinburgh was entering into a Golden Age which for nearly a century was to make her probably the pre-eminent cultural centre of the Western World. The Continent was ravaged by the French Revolution and the Napoleonic wars, North America was just beginning to find herself, and somehow conditions converged upon Edinburgh as the site for a remarkable flowering of learning and culture. In the words of Sydney Smith, a clergyman of the day,

> I like this place extremely and cannot help thinking that for a literary man . . . it is the most eligible situation in the island. It unites good Libraries liberally managed, learned men without any other system than that of pursuing truth, very good general society, large healthy virgins with mild pleasing countenances and white swelling breasts – shores washed by the sea – the romantic grandeur of antient and the beautiful regularity of modern building, and boundless floods of oxygen.[2]

Edinburgh's flowering encompassed an astonishing range of fields. As Douglas Young has pointed out, those whose activities were focused on Edinburgh included Sir Walter Scott the novelist, David Hume the philosopher, Adam Smith the economist, Robert Burns the poet, Robert Adam the architect, Henry Raeburn the painter, the creators of the first *Encyclopaedia Britannica*, the critics and reformers who wrote the *Edinburgh Review*, and leading medical men, scientists, town planners, lawyers, churchmen and others.

Life in Edinburgh in that period lacked many of the amenities which we take for granted today: there was no electricity or telephone or fax or Internet, there were no railways or motor cars or aircraft, and sanitation and public health and medicine were in a comparatively rudimentary state. But the spirit was there. Figuratively as well as literally there were boundless floods of oxygen and fresh air.

The concept of the intellectual has of late largely lost its meaning and has become confused with that of the specialist – whether the IT specialist or otherwise. The very term "intellectual" has fallen into disfavour. A form of inverted snobbery has come into play.

I now redefine the true intellectual as the multi-disciplinary man – or woman. I shall call the multidisciplinary man the new intellectual. Actually he is not new because he lives in a great tradition going back to the days of Aristotle and before. But now it is time for him to be rapidly rehabilitated. The new intellectual can, and will, reassert himself. I shall spell out his role as this book unfolds.

If there is anything that is boring it is what I can term the matter-of-fact old intellectual man – or woman. In the light of experience – especially in Russia but also in other places – I now further define the new intellectual as one having an inherent and in-built sense of humour. Only then can he deploy the imagination required to solve old and new problems in new ways. Humour and imagination go together.

The new intellectual will face challenges aplenty in dealing with, for example, multimedia madness. The pace of technological change is such that ordinary television viewers will soon be able to choose from among more than 400 channels.[3] This will offer superb opportunities for the couch potato – to use a term now widely recognized in the English language. It will provide him or her with a state of perfect bliss. And students of the media may likewise be able to enunciate a new law delineating an inverse relationship between the number of television channels and their quality.

Moreover, as a Microsoft senior vice president has forecast, "In the end, the computer and television will combine and become interchangeable."[4] The resources of the Internet will of course be incorporated and the citizen will enjoy wall-to-wall communications and computing coverage. Where will this lead?

David Shenk, in his *Data Smog: Surviving the Information Glut,* considers the implications. Information, he writes, "once rare and cherished like caviar, is plentiful and taken for granted like potatoes."[5] He refers to "the stagnation of American political knowledge over the past fifty years, even as Americans were formally educated to an unprecedented degree. We face a paradox of abundance-induced amnesia. The more information we come upon, the more we narrow our focus. The more we know, the less we know." And meanwhile the Internet has grown to where it contains some *eleven billion* words.[6]

"Superabundant information is grand," writes Shenk quoting Philip Novak, "until we understand that it can rob us of the peace that is our spiritual birthright."[7] Moreover, adds Shenk, "Books are the opposite of television. They are slow, engaging, inspiring, intellect-arousing, and creativity-spurring."[8] And amidst all the data smog, "a new kind of social responsibility has emerged – an obligation to be succinct."[9]

Laura Fillmore has employed the useful term "electronic servitude."[10] All of the eleven billion words on the Internet can be communicated – for better or for worse. As Shenk puts it, "Above all else, it is imperative that in the coming years we strive to keep the quality of our thinking as great as the quantity of our information."[11]

How does the ordinary man react to this glut of information? Too often he becomes hypnotized by it – and particularly by television, in its treatment of the world around us. This has reached the point where, in popular psychology, *nothing is real until we see it on television*. And "I saw it on television" becomes tantamount to saying that it is true. On the one hand this is in the realm of the couch potato but on the other hand it now universally affects modern man's thinking.

It is very important for us to reflect on the evolution of human communications – and for two reasons. In the first place, it illustrates communications technology in action over an extended period; and it exemplifies the interplay between felt needs and technological responses. In the second place, that evolution has deep philosopical significance.

The whole history of human communications illustrates the interaction between the seen and the unseen. For good reason the philosophy of science (my own original field) is much concerned with this subject – including both written and pictorial communications about unseen things. This has been a non-stop problem for both scientists and philosophers.

In man's evolution from the Stone Age to the Space Age, his means of communication have steadily evolved. Essential to this process was of course the early acquisition of rudimentary forms of language, including sign language and so-called body language. Ancient cave dwellers were among those who developed pictorial means of communication, and formalized alphabets and writing in due course evolved. In response to the problem of writing surfaces, stone, clay, wood, lead, copper and brass were among the materials employed, but these were heavy and bulky. Large leaves such as those of the palm might be utilized, but these were perishable.

Moreover, as Harry E. Neal points out, such materials as the foregoing made it virtually impossible for a scribe to make corrections or changes in his text. The early Romans came up with an ingenious solution to this problem. They coated flat pieces of wood with wax and cut their inscriptions into the wax. When alterations were required, they could smooth over the wax and make fresh inscriptions.[12] Thus the Romans had a two-way message system that was rather in the spirit of the present-day fax machine.

But it was the Egyptians who scored a great breakthrough with their development of papyrus writing paper. Papyrus is a tall-growing water plant which flourished in the shallow waters of the Nile and from which the Egyptians cut long narrow strips which they then interwove, soaked, pounded, dried in the sun, and smoothed with a piece of shell or stone. The result was a superb and durable writing surface of which many examples have survived for thousands of years. In spite of the use of different raw materials, the paper-making technology evolved by the ancient Egyptians has much in common with that of the modern multinational paper industry.

Men have long realized the importance of delivering written or other messages in minimum time. A shouted command or other oral message could be delivered promptly over a short distance, but long-range messaging called for more ingenuity. For example, in the days of the Persian empire (which at its height, about 500 BC, covered most of the present-day Middle East) royal couriers, using closely spaced relay stations with fresh horses at each, could span the empire within fifteen days; and chains of regularly spaced semaphore towers stretching across the countryside permitted even faster communication. Much later, the inventor Claude Chappe (1763–1805) developed an improved semaphore system which was first used at the time of the French Revolution; with the aid of towers built at suitable intervals he was able to send messages 450 miles from Paris to the fleet in Toulon in 20 minutes.[13]

The advent of the printing press of course greatly enhanced the scope of communication. It appears that the Chinese, as early as 868 AD, were the first to use movable type, in the shape of carved wooden blocks. It was not until about 1440 that movable type was apparently independently developed in Germany either by Johann Gutenberg or one of his associates, and the printing of the first of the famous Gutenberg Bibles seems to have been completed in about 1456. Some scholars claim that printing with movable type may have been developed in Holland at an earlier time, but in any event it spread very rapidly. In the Western world virtually all books were printed in Latin until about 1476, when in an historic development printing in English was introduced by William Caxton of Kent.

"The art of printing," as Neal remarks, "helped to bring the 'Dark Ages' of ignorance and superstition in Europe to an end. New ideas spread far and wide by means of the printed word."[14] Moreover it was printing, together with a whole range of additional communications technologies that were to come, which propelled the English language onto the world stage and increasingly gave it the role of the one principal universal language.

The interest in speeding up communication was to continue unabated, and this among other things led to incipient forms of postal services. As early as about 3800 BC, the then king of Babylon had entrusted "letters," in the shape of inscribed clay tablets, to relays of runners who carried them across the country. In the fifth century BC, Herodotus, the Greek historian, wrote as follows about men on horseback who carried messages inscribed on bronze tablets: "Neither snow, nor rain, nor heat, nor gloom of night stays these couriers from the swift completion of their appointed rounds."[15] Much later, the US postal service embraced this as its official motto.

The Emperor Diocletian inaugurated a limited postal service in Rome around 300 AD; but after Rome's fall the concept lapsed and it was not until the sixteenth century that proper public postal services were established in France, Germany, and Britain. In 1784 England's first mail-coach was started; the coach ran between London and Bristol and covered the nearly 120 miles in sixteen hours. But faster means of communication were desired, and the need soon called forth new technology.

In 1825 a steam locomotive, designed and built by George Stephenson, hauled both passengers and mail at the astonishing speed of twelve miles per hour. This was the beginning of the vast railway industry, with tracks spanning many parts of the globe and with the carrying of mail as one of its key roles. In 1918 the world's first regular air-mail service was established between Washington, DC and New York City.[16] But electrical and electronic means had already been recognized as offering far more scope for high-speed messaging.

Communication took a great leap forward with the invention of the electric telegraph, especially the version perfected by Samuel F. B. Morse, an American portrait artist turned technologist. In 1844 Morse and his team completed construction of a telegraph line between Washington and Baltimore, and over it was sent, in Morse code, the famous message, "What hath God wrought?" This was the first message sent over the first public telegraph line in the world, and the use of the telegraph soon spread by leaps and bounds. Submarine telegraphy before long began in earnest, with a cable being laid under the English Channel in 1851 and a transatlantic cable being completed in 1866.[17] These cables carried telegraphic messages by wire and soon it would become possible to send likenesses of the human voice as well.

The principal inventor of the telephone was of course Alexander Graham Bell, a Scotsman who had migrated to Boston, Massachusetts. In 1876 Bell and his assistant Thomas A. Watson obtained a US patent for the instrument, which later in that same year was exhibited at the Philadelphia Centennial Exhibition. In 1878, while on a honeymoon trip to England, Bell was invited to demonstrate his invention to Queen Victoria, who was so taken with it that she had a private line installed from the Isle of Wight to London. A few months later the world's first general telephone service began operations in London.[18]

My father knew Alexander Graham Bell and visited him at his home. The great inventor told my father that he would never consider having a telephone in his house; he would find it too distracting. Perhaps he had a premonition about information overload!

Although the telephone soon became a phenomenal success, men had already been groping for some way to achieve the rapid transmission of messages over long distances without wires. In 1894 Guglielmo Marconi, the Italian inventor, who was then only twenty years old, began experiments aimed at sending messages without wires. In the following year he succeeded in sending crude radio signals over two miles. He then took his findings to London and to Britain's Post Office Telegraph Department. Sir William Preece, the director of that department, displayed remarkably non-bureaucratic behaviour when in 1897 he arranged for Marconi to give a demonstration of his invention before a group of government officials. Before a distinguished audience Marconi showed that he could send clear electrical signals over a distance of several hundred yards without wires.

At the request of the Italian navy, Marconi then installed his radio equipment in some of their warships and showed that he could send messages between ships twelve miles apart. Then came the great challenge, for he was deter-mined to try to send radio messages across the Atlantic from Cornwall to Newfoundland. This he managed to do in 1901, using a receiving aerial suspended some 400 feet in the air from a kite.[19]

The age of long-distance radio communication could be fairly said to have begun.

Marconi of course sent his early radio messages by Morse code, but soon it became possible to employ the human voice as well. Numerous scientists and inventors had a hand in the development of radio broadcasting, and notable among these was Lee DeForest, who perfected and patented the radio tube or valve which permitted great amplification of weak radio signals. Although there is considerable dispute as to when the human voice was first broadcast by radio, it is known that a Christmas Eve broadcast of talk and music took place in Massachusetts in 1906; that British Navy tech-nicians transmitted "God Save the King" from one ship to another in 1907; and that DeForest broadcast a performance from the Metropolitan Opera House in New York in 1910. The first commercially licensed radio station was KDKA in

Pittsburgh, which commenced operations in 1920, and in Britain the first such station went on air in 1922.[20]

Contributing to the dramatic worldwide spread of radio broadcasting has of course been the transistor as invented by a team at the Bell Telephone Laboratories in 1948. It has permitted far more compact and durable radio broadcasting and receiving equipment, and cheap transistor radios are now found on every part of the planet regardless of the prevailing political or social system. The transistor likewise played a key role in the field of television including broadcasting by satellite.

A number of pioneers, whose work dates back even to the nineteenth century, helped pave the way to television. In 1915 Marconi forecast that there would one day be a "visible telephone." But the greatest of the television pioneers was undoubtedly a Scottish parson's son named John Logie Baird. In 1925, in London, he actually transmitted the likeness of a human face from one room to an adjoining room. Three years later, from Baird's studio, the British Broadcasting Corporation made the world's first public television broadcast. The BBC continued with experimental broadcasts and in 1936 it launched the first regular public television service in the world. This landmark was to have enormous political and cultural repercussions of which we are still only beginning to be properly aware.

These early broadcasts were of course in black and white, and inventors had meanwhile been trying to develop colour television. After initial encouraging experiments by Baird in Britain, the Bell Telephone Laboratories in 1929 sent colour television pictures over a wire in New York. In 1940 two other American companies made test colour television broadcasts,[21] and broadcasting in colour gradually spread throughout the world.

When in 1957 the Russians launched Sputnik I, the

world's first communications satellite, that revolutionary event followed many centuries of trial and experimentation. Rockets were first used for military purposes by the Chinese in about 1100 AD and were encountered by British forces in India in the eighteenth century. In the nineteenth century rockets found extensive use by various European armies; and in the first half of the twentieth century an especially devastating form of rocket was the V2 with its one-ton warhead as used by the Germans to attack the London area in the Second World War.

Concurrently Arthur C. Clarke, a brilliant British radar expert, was clearly delineating the concept of sending rocket-launched communications satellites into outer space in order to extend the reach of television broadcasting. He pointed out that three such satellites, correctly spaced in "stationary" orbit in relation to the earth's rotation, could provide global television coverage. Because the transistor had not yet been invented, Clarke visualized the need for very large satellites manned by crews to replace defective tubes or valves.[22] But in fact, as we have seen, the transistor was to be unveiled very soon afterwards and unmanned communications satellites became entirely feasible.

Sputnik I represented not only the world's first satellite but also the first man-made object ever to be launched into outer space. It indeed heralded the advent of the space age. Little imagination is required to discern that the traditional concept of the commanding heights now refers in large measure to space and the man-made vehicles that operate in space.

The proliferation of man-made satellites in outer space has been nothing less than phenomenal. By 1987 some 3500 military and civilian satellites were already in orbit and since then the number has grown apace. According to Mark Long, "satellites have forever altered the common perception of the world. . . ." Our planet, he adds, "is encircled by a ring of man-made satellites that generate an invisible electromagnetic web. This web bonds our world together with a continuous exchange of video, audio, and data information."[23]

The Russians astounded the world when they launched Sputnik I, and the repercussions have been felt ever since in the shape of profound national and international cultural consequences. It was Marshall McLuhan who, in a book first published in 1964, propounded the celebrated thesis that "the medium is the message."[24] He was of course referring primarily to the terrestrial electronic media of his day, and his argument was widely regarded as simplistic. With the dramatic subsequent growth of man's extraterrestrial activities, and with communication having acquired new spatial dimensions, one could be tempted to think that the McLuhan thesis contains more than a germ of truth.

A gifted and acclaimed researcher on the mass media and kindred topics, McLuhan detected that the nature of the mass media, particularly the electronic media, influenced the content of what was being disseminated. Yet as Philip Marchand, McLuhan's perceptive biographer, has shown, McLuhan's views on these matters remained ambivalent.

McLuhan, early in his career, condemned advertising, industrialism and big business not to mention Marxism. He became increasingly impressed with the way in which technological change could affect all aspects of human existence, and he focused especially on communications technology. Later he was to contend that his theory of change, which emphasized the means of communication rather than those of production, would supersede Marxism.[25] Meanwhile he was arguing that modern instantaneous communications bombarded people with impressions that made the world seem irrational rather than logical or literate. As Marchand notes, "Powerful gadgets like television were all the more dangerous, in McLuhan's view, because they fascinated those who used them and often turned those users into dependents." McLuhan even went so far as to state that he wished "none of those technologies ever happened."

Yet, suggests Marchand, McLuhan "certainly would never have maintained that there was anything intrinsically evil about technology or media. . . . One simply had to be very careful about using the media, and therefore one had to understand how the media really worked. . . ."[26] McLuhan even suggested that mankind may be on the verge of a great global culture. But increasingly, as Marchand points out, "McLuhan was struck by what he considered the absence of any overall theory of communication. . . ."[27]

McLuhan deserves much credit for having identified the lack of any proper interdisciplinary theory of communication. Particularly after the satellite revolution engendered by Sputnik I, such an intellectual discrepancy becomes all the more glaring. It arises from a certain naivety which still prevails today and which leads to many errors of judgement.

But the root of the problem goes much deeper. As we shall see later in this book, it has to do with *the nature of fundamental reality*. This is a subject full of fascination.

In the next chapter we shall deal with pragmatic syndrome, the disease which afflicts so much Western thought, particularly in America. Those who have the disease try to judge each case on its own supposed merits without any guiding principles or framework. As a foretaste of what is to follow we can consider an American disaster of epic proportions.

The Vietnam War represented by far the worst military or military/political defeat in the history of the United States of America. It traumatized America and it left deep and lasting scars particularly among the young. Moreover, that defeat contrasted sharply with the decisive victory won not long before by Britain and her Malayan allies against the Communists. Besides, that famous victory took place almost next door to Vietnam.

A few years ago I was the house guest, in Kuala Lumpur, of a British major general. We used to sit on his veranda overlooking his beautiful tropical garden; and one of the subjects we discussed was the radically different approaches employed by the British during the Malayan Emergency on the one hand and by the Americans in Vietnam on the other. Our conversations, in such a peaceful setting in a country which had formerly seen so much violence, were very revealing.

As Sir Robert Thompson points out in his *Defeating Communist Insurgency*, it was early in 1948, on instructions from Moscow, that the Communists in Southeast Asia gave orders for a major offensive; and their primary initial target was Malaya.[28] Thus began the Malayan Emergency. The Communists launched terrorism on a wide scale, both among the native Malayan population and among expatriates. Many British planters and businessmen were assassinated, and the economy rapidly deteriorated. Things went from bad to worse.

It was not until 1952 that London sent out a brilliant interdisciplinarian in the shape of General (subsequently Field Marshal) Sir Gerald Templer, who was to become known as the Tiger of Malaya. Soon after his arrival in Malaya he wrote the following statement which succinctly expressed his strategic philosophy: "The shooting side of the business is only 25% of the trouble and the other 75% lies in getting the people of this country behind us."[29]

His successful interdisciplinary strategy comprized three principal elements. The first was low-intensity warfare – in contrast to the massive bombardments, by the mighty B52 bombers and otherwise, which were let loose by the Americans in Vietnam and which largely served to alienate the indigenous populace. The second was a strong ideological initiative to win over the hearts and minds of the people, even including the terrorists themselves. The third was a well-formulated and well-explained programme of economic and political development, which would help bring economic recovery and would provide hope for the future.

Altogether the Malayan Emergency lasted for twelve years, from June, 1948 to July, 1960.[30] The first four years, until General Templer's arrival, were a period of drift and deterioration. But then his multidisciplinary genius was to transform everything. Patience and persistence were required but then the victory, when it came, was complete and decisive.

The contrast with America's subsequent performance in Vietnam could hardly be more dramatic. It is true that the Communists in Malaya were mostly Chinese in origin and were therefore somewhat alien to the Malays, whereas in Vietnam the Communists were mostly Vietnamese. It is also true that it was much easier to police the borders of peninsular Malaya than those of Vietnam. But those points having been made, the great defect in America's intervention in Vietnam was that she lacked any multidisciplinary strategic vision. Objectively speaking the American defeat was therefore completely inevitable.

America's costly involvement in the Vietnam War indeed proved thoroughly non-productive. By the end of 1968 America had over 500,000 servicemen in Vietnam and she had actually dropped a heavier tonnage of bombs on North Vietnam than fell on Germany and Japan put together in the entire Second World War.[31] Yet the United States and her South Vietnamese allies were to suffer horrible casualties and an ignominious defeat.

If, on the other hand, America had properly learned from

General Templer and his team, the results would have been very different. An inspired and patient and persistent multi-disciplinary strategy would have paid off – even if, as in Malaya, it took twelve years, or eight years if we reckon from the date when Templar took charge. Besides, as we shall see later in this book, it was soon to become apparent that Marxism-Leninism contained the seeds of its own destruction and that the Soviet Union would collapse.

That was to change everything, in Southeast Asia and throughout the world. And now, in the next chapter, we shall see how to escape from the kind of straight-jacketed thinking that led to America's disastrous defeat in Vietnam and that without due care could lead to yet other catastrophes in the future.

II The Pragmatic Fixation

When US President Bill Clinton's woman troubles were reaching a climax in 1998, his wife Hillary publicly declared that the whole thing had arisen from "a vast right-wing conspiracy."[1] But because of America's so-called pragmatic tradition, most Americans had only the foggiest idea of what that meant. The couch potato's view of the whole affair was all too characteristic.

Indeed, most Americans had no idea where the term "pragmatism," in its philosophical sense, had come from in the first place. Meanwhile many politicians, particularly in America and Britain, have habitually and with obvious pride referred to their "pragmatic" approach to public affairs. The same term has come to be widely employed among literary critics, media men, and others, many of whom have never inquired into its origins or precise implications. For the moment it is sufficient to note that, as one source expresses it, "The word 'pragmatism' was very little used in the English language, and not at all in philosophical contexts, until it was introduced by the American philosopher C. S. Peirce in 1878 as the name of a logical maxim for determining the meaning of words which he had formulated."[2] Later the term became a generalized piece of popular jargon.

Peirce did not at all intend that the word should signify a complete philosophical position, but William James, John Dewey and others borrowed and distorted the term and gave it the flavour of a full-blown philosophy. In due course, as J. O. Urmson points out, the word "became a name for any position which lays emphasis on results as a test for satisfactoriness."[3]

In its corrupted and popularized form, pragmatism thus came to mean judging any proposed course of action by the following rule: it is good if it works. But what about successfully robbing a bank in order to solve one's financial problems, and what about courses of action that might "work" in the short term but perhaps not in the longer term? Practical pragmatists tended to avoid such esoteric considerations and to opt in favour of what seemed uncomplicated common-sense notions of what works.

As Morton White suggests in his *Pragmatism and the American Mind*, pragmatism became "the most distinctive American philosophical movement,"[4] and in contagious fashion it spread into the popular culture. American politicians, business executives and others felt complimented rather than insulted when they were called good pragmatists. To modify Marx, one could say that pragmatism rather than religion became the opiate of the people – not only in the United States but also in many other countries influenced by her culture.

In earlier days in America, the practical trial-and-error approach had seemed well suited to the needs of a relatively simple technology and society, but even then it had been tempered by the strong religious impulses of the time. With the advent of the twenty-first century, one found a very different situation. The pragmatic outlook readily leads to intellectual traps such as that symbolized by the American disaster in Vietnam.

What can be called The Fallacy of the Parochial Context finds useful illustration in the relationship between modern technology and the natural environment. Consider, for example, automobiles and jet planes: they work. Consider chemical fertilizers and insecticides: they work. Consider strip mining: it works. Consider nuclear weapons: they work. But in each of those cases what works in the parochial sense may in wider terms carry serious potential hazards. In an ever-growing number of instances we find that only through a national or global environmental outlook can we really assess what works.

The pragmatic test has indeed become a fertile source of mistaken decisions and counter-productive policies. Clearly the new intellectual, as we have identified him in the previous chapter, must *become the post-pragmatic intellectual.* His post-pragmatic role will be to approach problems with a wide-ranging and far-ranging multidisciplinary outlook.

The emergence of the post-pragmatic outlook can best be understood by briefly examining intellectual trends since 1960. It was in that year that Daniel Bell published his famous *The End of Ideology,*[5] with a revised edition following in 1962. To a remarkable degree the book managed to forecast and capture the spirit of what historians may some day characterize as the Simplistic Sixties; even the book's very title struck an instant responsive chord with many people who had never read it or even seen it. For it seemed to suggest an end to old dogmas and outworn creeds and a refreshing new reliance upon practical pragmatic experience.

Ideology, declared Bell in his book, "which once was a road to action, has come to a dead end." A social movement, he went on to explain, "can rouse people when it can do three things: simplify ideas, establish a claim to truth and, in the union of the two, demand a commitment to action.

Thus, not only does ideology transform ideas, it transforms people as well."

"Ideology," explained Bell, "is the conversion of ideas into levers. What gives ideologies their force is their passion; in this sense they become secular religions." But today, Bell assured his readers, such ideologies – including Marxism – "are exhausted."

Bell conceded "the extraordinary fact" that "the rising states of Asia and Africa are fashioning new ideologies" including those of "industrialization, modernization, Pan-Arabism, color, and nationalism." But he regarded these ideologies as "parochial, instrumental, and created by political leaders. . . . The impulsions of the new ideologies are economic development and national power."[6]

As his title indicates, Bell's whole treatment – and the easy assumptions of most of his contemporaries in the sixties and onwards – suggested that the days of widely-held and powerful ideologies were over. In a later and more satisfactory book entitled *The Coming of Post-Industrial Society*, Bell comments as follows:

> For most of human history, *reality was nature*, and in poetry and imagination men sought to relate the self to the natural world. Then *reality becomes technics*, tools and things made by man yet given an independent existence outside himself. . . . Now *reality is primarily the social world* – neither nature nor things, only men – experienced through the reciprocal consciousness of self and others. Society itself becomes a web of consciousness, . . . to be realized as a social construction. . . .[7]

This was fine as far as it went, but the ideological element was still missing. The same problem applies with Alvin Toffler's widely-distributed *Future Shock*, which was first published in 1970 and has gone through many editions since.[8]

This was followed by a sequel called *The Third Wave*,[9] a study of so-called post-industrial culture. Although each of these books runs to more than 500 pages and both of them carry voluminous indexes, astonishingly neither index contains a single entry on ideology or philosophy. They both demonstrate the pragmatic illusion.

Still another book reflecting the pragmatic viewpoint is Charles A. Reich's *The Greening of America*,[10] which was first published in 1970, the same year as the first edition of Toffler's *Future Shock*. As in the previous two instances, the work seemed to describe and foretell the emerging mood of the world or at least a significant part of it extending far beyond the United States.

A revolution, declares Reich, is coming. "It will not be like the revolutions of the past. It will originate with the individual and with culture, and it will change the political structure only as its final act."

"This," he says, "is the revolution of the new generation. . . . It is both necessary and inevitable, and in time it will include not only youth, but all people in America."[11] Reich then develops his famous trilogy of Consciousness I, II, and III.

Consciousness I, he explains, "believes that the American dream is still possible, and that success is determined by character, morality, hard work, and self-denial."[12] Consciousness II, represents a logical evolution from I. "Believing that the best and most hopeful part of man is his gift of reason, Consciousness II seeks to design a world in which reason will prevail." At the heart of Consciousness II "is the insistence that what man produces by means of reason – the state, laws, technology, manufactured goods – constitute the true reality. Just as Consciousness I centers on the fiction of the American Adam, the competitive struggle, and the triumph of the virtuous and strong individual, so Consciousness II rests on the fiction of logic and machinery; what it considers unreal is nature and subjective man.''[13]

Consciousness III, on the other hand, ''starts with self. In contrast to Consciousness II, which accepts society, the public interest, and institutions as the primary reality, III declares that the individual self is the only true reality.'' Furthermore, Consciousness III rejects the whole concept of excellence and comparative merit that is so central to Consciousness II.

The emphasis upon self expresses itself in a number of ways, not least in modes of dress – blue jeans, neuter unisex styles, and all the rest. Next we come to the rock and associated music of Consciousness III, which provides ''the chief medium of expression, the chief means by which inner feelings are communicated.''[14] Then we come to marijuana and other psychedelic drugs, which Reich recommends as ''truth serum'' and among ''the most important means of restoring dulled consciousness.''[15]

Consciousness III, asserts Reich,

is utterly different from I and II. It seeks restoration of the non-material elements of man's existence, the elements like the natural environment and the spiritual that were passed by in the rush for material development. It seeks to transcend science and technology, to restore them to their proper place as tools of man rather than as determinants of man's existence.[16]

And he contends that it is through Consciousness III that one solves the psychological problem of alienation.

Reich, and the attitudes he symbolizes, have had a tremendous impact not only in America but also in many other parts of the world, and most of all among students – students who spoke in many languages but thought that they had found a common language in the new consciousness. Moreover, many men, even if they feel contempt for Reich's approach to life, will yet sympathize with his efforts to restore the non-material elements of man's existence and to transcend science and technology and restore them to their proper place as tools rather than determinants.

One may perhaps ask whether his path provides the most direct route to the realization of those aims. As Arnold J. Wolf has expressed it,

> The dream of the New Consciousness was a lovely dream which is now sadly over. We have to begin again in that world which is all around us, as well as within us. . . . Our world is still unredeemed. It is perilous. Messiah has not yet come. The young are not the Messiah. . . . The revolution will not come as we watch it on our television sets. There is no hiding place. . . . The young are neither our saviours nor our enemies. They are our successors and our children.[17]

Still another widely-known approach is that of Francis Fukuyama, notably in his *The End of History and the Last Man*,[18] which was first published in book form in 1992. Here the argument is not that ideologies are unimportant but that there is now such general agreement on ideologies that the subject no longer needs discussion. The argument is a seductive yet, as we shall see, a highly dangerous one.

In 1989, well before the appearance of Fukuyama's book, Zbigniew Brzezinski published a work with this resounding title: *The Grand Failure: The Birth and Death of Communism in the Twentieth Century*.[19] In the book he described how, in tune with the then-collapsing Soviet Union, the world was witnessing an ever-widening democratic consensus. But Fukuyama carried the argument further in terms of the historical process itself.

In a rambling and discursive treatment he argued that

A remarkable consensus concerning the legitimacy of liberal democracy as a system of government had emerged throughout the world in the past few years, as it conquered rival ideologies like hereditary monarchy, fascism, and most recently communism. More than that, however, . . . liberal democracy may constitute 'the end point of mankind's ideological evolution' and 'the final form of human government,' and as such constituted the 'end of history.'[20]

According to Fukuyama, while earlier forms of government contained "grave defects and irrationalities" that led eventually to their demise, liberal democracy was "arguably free from such internal contradictions." He concedes that in the United States and other stable democracies injustice and serious social problems are still to be found; but he claims that such problems arise only from "incomplete implementation of the twin principles of liberty and equality."[21]

This reminds me of an experience a few years ago in Russia, in the magnificent city of St. Petersburg – then known grotesquely as Leningrad. I was asked to take part in a debate on Marxism-Leninism to be held at the Lenin Museum, which was housed in a large and beautiful pre-revolutionary palace. One of those taking part in the debate was a young lady curator with fiery red hair and a fiery disposition. She confronted me with this question: would you not agree that Marxism-Leninism is a perfect system and that any seeming flaws in the system are purely a matter of improper implementation?

To her chagrin I replied that the system itself contained fundamental ideological flaws which even the most efficient implementation could never cure. The sequel was that, with growing public awareness, the Lenin Museum was soon afterwards closed forever.

Later in this book we shall return to the fate and future of Marxism-Leninism. But for the moment the analogy is clear. Liberal democracy is a wonderful system, but it is also a system that faces severe and dangerous challenges as we move into the dawning century. A pragmatic end-of-ideology response provides the perfect way to invite fresh disasters such as that which befell the Americans in Vietnam.

It is interesting that Fukuyama leaves a gaping hole in his own argument when he considers the power and influence of Islam. As he himself expresses it,

> It is true that Islam constitutes a systematic and coherent ideology. . . . The appeal of Islam is universal, reaching out to all men. . . . And Islam has indeed defeated liberal democracy in many parts of the Islamic world, posing a grave threat to liberal practices even in countries where it has not achieved political power directly. . . .
> Despite the power demonstrated by Islam in its current revival, . . . it remains the case that this religion has virtually no appeal outside those areas that were culturally Islamic to begin with. The days of Islamic cultural conquests, it would seem, are over. . . . And while nearly a billion people are culturally Islamic – one-fifth of the world's population – they cannot challenge liberal democracy on its own territory on the level of ideas. . . .[22]

This is far from necessarily being the case. Islam has a long and successful history of proselytizing. Moreover, radical or fundamentalist Islam has shown a remarkable ability to ride roughshod over Islamic moderates, as I have seen at first hand.

For four years I was on the faculty of the University of Tehran; and there, on that beautiful campus, with snow-capped mountains looming overhead even on hot summer days, I and colleagues created Iran's pioneering Institute for Public and Business Administration. I had brilliant and highly-motivated students who were keen to help with their country's modernization; but ideological considerations were later to intervene.

Likewise, in the latter 1950s, I served as personal advisor to the late Shah of Iran, Mohammed Reza Shah Pahlavi. The Shah made remarkable contributions to his country's development, and these are well recorded in his memoirs entitled *Mission for My Country*.[23]

The Shah's father, Reza Shah Pahlavi, had an astonishing record in modernizing his country, and his relations with the Islamic clergy were always prickly. As his son expressed it,

Because he was always hounding certain sections of the clergy, many people thought that he was not religious; but I know that is untrue. He pushed the clergy into the background because at that time many of them were hindering the country's progress and interfering too much in affairs of state. If one had not treated them somewhat roughly, it might have taken three or four times as long as it did to carry out his programme of modernizing the country.[24]

And the son related that on one occasion, after some priests had insulted his wife for not wearing the veil (which the Shah had banned), the Shah personally invaded the mosque with his boots on and horse-whipped the offending priests.

Continuing with his father's work in modernizing the country, the son inaugurated a whole series of measures including, for example, his Literacy Corps which sent teachers to villages all over the country. Among his most fundamental measures were his land reforms, which gave ownership of agricultural land to millions of ordinary farmers throughout Iran.[25] The land-distribution programme was carried out in three stages: first, royal land; secondly, government land; and thirdly, private land. When it came to the third stage, it turned out that much of the appropriated private land was owned by the clergy; and they swore eternal vengeance for this seeming sacrilege.

Already, under the Shah's leadership, the Iranian economy was growing rapidly and modernization was proceeding apace. In 1971, I attended the glittering celebrations marking the 2500th anniversary of the Iranian monarchy, with heavy emphasis properly being laid on Iran's pre-Islamic as well as Islamic culture. Meanwhile the Shah asked me to return to his country as an advisor; but because of other commitments I did not, and subsequently I kicked myself, because I could have warned him about some of the looming dangers – especially those connected with Westernization.

In 1978–79 came the Iranian Revolution, which carried, and continues to carry, profound implications for all Islamic communities and for the world at large. According to Sir Anthony Parsons, Britain's ambassador to Iran during the most turbulent period of that revolution, "the scale of the political earthquake . . . was equal to, if it did not surpass, that of the two great revolutions of modern European history, the French and the Russian." But he adds that what took place was actually not so much a revolution as a counter-revolution – and one that effectively meant retrogression to the sociopolitical structure of more than half a century before. Likewise he adds that many of those who took part in, or acquiesced in, that counter-revolution "must now be filled with boundless regret."[26]

In the years leading up to the Iranian Revolution, the Shah, albeit with the best of intentions, made grave errors in three major categories: the response to communism, the response to Islam, and the response to Western economic and cultural values. Having the then Soviet Union as his neighbour, it was natural that he should be concerned with the menace of communism. Accordingly, with oil money and with American military aid and advice, the Shah obtained huge quantities of heavy weapons designed to protect his country from the Soviet threat – and by implication from the threat of radical Islam as well. Under American influence – with the same sort of end-of-ideology mentality that had already provided guidance during the American debacle in Vietnam – the Shah and his advisors gave insufficient attention to the ideological problems posed by Marxism on the one hand and by Islamic extremism on the other.

In the field of Islam, the Shah was recognized as a devout Muslim and the Ayatollah Khomeini, as revolutionary leader, could scarcely claim superiority in this respect. Ironically it was partly with the aim of offsetting communism that the Shah had given much money for the building of mosques and for religious education. But he and his advisors signally failed to understand or to counteract the powerful ideology that was brewing in the minds of the radical Moslems. This helped to guarantee the inevitability of the Islamic extremist explosion that was to come.

With regard to Western economic and cultural values, Iran under the Shah attained some of the world's highest economic growth rates; and then, in the early 1970s, came the quadrupling of world oil prices with vast cash benefits for oil-rich Iran. This prompted the Shah to order a still further acceleration of the national economic development programme.

Under such pressure, existing logistical and other bottlenecks worsened and fresh ones appeared; but this was not the main point. The Shah and his economic advisors had tragically failed to take into proper account *the cultural side-effects* of rapid economic growth. The cultural problem, already serious before the acceleration, became even worse after it. Big Western-style capital-intensive projects had been largely favoured; and increasingly the ordinary Iranian felt like a bystander in his own country. Western films and the uncritical emulation of Western ways, particularly among the young, proved deeply disturbing to Iranians who cherished the values of their own traditional culture.

The Shah was thoroughly devoted to modern – i.e., largely Western – education, and with a truly religious fervour he sought to bring it to all of his people. He rapidly expanded elementary education, including his Literacy Corps, and he lavished countless millions of dollars on building up the system of high schools, technical schools and colleges, and universities.

The Shah, in his zeal to modernize his country with utmost speed, gave an unstinting welcome to Western technology and to all the paraphernalia of what has so rapidly become the world's science-based culture. People with religious sensibilities – mainstream moderates as well as the more fanatical elements – watched with horror as the country's own ancient culture became increasingly inundated with Western films and television programmes, pop music carried by cheap transistor radios to the remotest areas of that large country, and Western curricular concepts. They were aghast to see girl students reduced to promiscuity on the fine new university campuses and to witness the dissolution of family traditions and the rapid rise of divorce. Thus the Shah unwittingly played into the hands of the extremists, who soon unleashed a ferocious revolution.

Most Iranians, who pride themselves on not being Arabs, belong to the Shia branch of Islam as distinct from the Sunni branch found chiefly in the Arab world. The Shias have always been known as the branch of protest and revolution, and we could say that in the crisis of 1978–79 Iranians fully lived up to their reputation.

The ensuing decade witnessed almost unbelievable retrogression. The war with Iraq was a disaster. The regime's human rights record was a disaster. The economy was in a state of disaster. Culturally the country atrophied. But then very gradually the regime began to moderate its policies and to seek rapprochement with the West.

Worldwide, Islam possesses enormous vitality by virtue of the fact that it offers *a powerful multi-disciplinary outlook and system.* Under Islam, there is *no distinction between the secular and the spiritual.*[27] As Harrie and Chippindale have expressed it,

> Unlike Christianity, Islam could never become a private religion of personal conscience and ethics. Rather it is a complete way of life governing dress, economics, business ethics, rates of taxation, justice and punishment, weights and measures, politics, war and peace, marriage and inheritance, family and domestic life, the care of animals and livestock, sexual relations within marriage, education, diet, cookery, social behaviour, forms of greeting and rules of hospitality. Even the way a glass of water is to be drunk is governed by religious law.[28]

So why, with such potency, should Islam not take over the world? In the latter part of the seventeenth century, Europeans no doubt asked just such a question. For in September, 1683 a huge Ottoman Moslem army actually reached the gates of Vienna before finally being driven back.[29] Islam then went into a long and gentle decline. But in recent decades it has shown vastly increased vitality. Although Christianity still has more nominal believers worldwide than does Islam, Islam may have more true believers.

There are some 48 nations in the world where Muslims have an undisputed majority of the inhabitants,[30] and the number of such nations seems likely to increase for the time being.

The Koran is a beautifully-written book, rather poetic in nature and containing a wealth of precepts and injunctions such as the following:

> Woe to those who pray but are heedless in their prayer; who make a show of piety and give no alms to the destitute. . . .
> Would that you knew what the Height is! It is the freeing of a bondsman; the feeding, in the day of famine, of an orphaned relation or a needy man in distress; to have faith and to enjoin fortitude and mercy. . . .
> We have enjoined man to show kindness to his parents. . . . Inspire me, Lord to give thanks for the favours You have bestowed on me and on my parents, and to do good works that will please You. . . .
> Do not treat men with scorn. . . . Allah does not love the arrogant and the vainglorious. Rather let your gait be modest and your voice low: the harshest of voices is the braying of the ass. . . .
> . . . . Give just weight and measure and do not defraud others of their possessions. . . .
> Allah has now revealed the best of scriptures, a book uniform in style proclaiming promises and warnings. . . . He bestows it on whom he will.[31]

Complementing and supplementing *The Koran* is a large body of Islamic law known as the Sharia. It is an all-embracing legal system relating to every aspect of life.[32] As Bernard Lewis indicates, Islam is a system both of faith and of state, society, law, thought, and art.[33] It is this which justifies the statement that under Islam there is no distinction between the religious and the secular; they constitute a seamless web.

Christianity, arguably the greatest of all the world religions, is sharply different. In most Western countries a careful distinction is made between church and state and between the religious and the secular. The upshot is that at times when Western secular ideologies are weak and flabby, that tends to weaken the church and the Christian faith as well. This downward spiral can help to explain what many people regard as the West's cultural malaise.

Closely linked with the Western end-of-ideology psychology or psychosis has been the appearance of a strange animal called value-free analysis. As Brian Easlea has well summarized the posture,

> The proponents of value-free social science believe that there is complete identity between the natural and social sciences. Just as the natural scientist aims at understanding the physical world without passing judgement on whether or not, for example, the law of gravity should or should not be what it is, so the social scientist must aim at understanding the social world without passing judgement on the various societies, institutions, and social practices he is studying. The only legitimate aim of social science is to understand what *is*, not what *could be or should be*. The only value judgement allowed, therefore, is that value-judgement should be excluded.[34]

This statement provides a fitting indicator of where the pragmatic addiction has led us. We can do much better.

Intellectuals, particularly those in the West, must shake themselves out of their lethargy and their confusion. And what should be the role of the new post-pragmatic intellectual in this process? He must show that he can assimilate moral and spiritual values. He must prove that the end-of-ideology and end-of-history psychosis can be quickly superseded. He must demonstrate that he is capable of leadership in the post-pragmatic age.

For these things to happen, careful preparation is necessary, and for this we shall follow a well-delineated route. As a next step we must consider the vast and in some ways triumphant role of modern science and technology, extending all over the Planet Earth and well beyond Earth as well. How can we inject ideological elements and values into the scientific process? Then we shall examine lessons to be learned from the greatest and most disastrous "scientific" experiment in human history to date: that imposed in the Soviet Union as the world's first major Marxist state. After that we shall continue the analysis as it leads towards a new post-pragmatic ideology.

III Giants of Science

As Anita Phillips suggests in her perceptive book entitled *A Defence of Masochism*, "artists are nothing if not *professional* [her italics] masochists. . . . Artists are productive masochists."[1] This is a profound observation which helps to distinguish creative minds from ordinary minds. Here she is referring to emotional or spiritual masochism, but later in this book we shall take up the question of physical masochism.

A creative writer is an artist. As a professional writer all his life, my father among other things published a highly successful book on writing. As he pointed out in the book, ". . . In the last resort, *all* writers *must* go it alone, since writing is one of the most individual and personal of attitudes and activities."[2] And all gifted writers are productive masochists.

The same principle applies to gifted scientists; and here a prime example is Isaac Newton (1642–1727), who is commonly regarded as history's greatest scientist thus far, and who for most of his life was linked to the University of Cambridge. In Michael White's characterization of Newton in his *Isaac Newton: The Last Sorcerer*,

What has been gradually revealed is the image of a genius who sought knowledge in everything he came across, a man who

35

was driven to investigate all facets of life he encountered, everything that puzzled him. Such voraciousness drove him to self-inflicted injury, nervous breakdown, to a state in which he almost lost his mind, and possibly even to occult practices and the black arts. But the work that emerged from these explorations changed the world.[3]

Near the Great Gate of Trinity College, Cambridge, where Newton had his rooms, there stands an apple tree directly descended from the Newton tree that grew in the garden of Woolsthorpe Manor, Newton's Lincolnshire home some sixty miles from Cambridge. Sir Isaac's friend William Stukeley gave the following account of a conversation in which Newton had explained to him how the fall of an apple from that tree had helped to inspire a major new scientific concept:

> After dinner the weather being warm, we went into the garden and drank thea, only he and myself. Amidst other discourse, he told me, he was just in the same situation, as when formerly the notion of gravitation came into his mind. It was occasioned by the fall of an apple, as he sat in contemplative mood. Why should that apple always descend perpendicularly to the ground, thought he to himself. Why should it not go sideways or upwards? . . .[4]

Thus arose, in the mind of a genius, the principle of universal gravitation. In the chapel of Trinity College there rests a statue of Newton that inspired the poet Wordsworth to write

Of Newton with the prism and silent face,
The marble index of a mind for ever
Voyaging through strange seas of thought, alone.

Newton's whole life illustrated the intimate interplay between the theoretical and the practical. When Newton was only nine years old he carved a sundial from a block of stone. As a schoolboy he used all available pocket money to buy tools for model-making. Among other things he constructed a water clock and a miniature windmill that could also operate on power supplied by a mouse. Young Newton startled the local inhabitants by sending a paper lantern aloft at night attached to the tail of a kite. He constructed overshot and undershot water wheels and performed various hydraulic experiments.

As the boy matured and went on to Cambridge, his irrepressible practical inventiveness did not desert him. Visiting Stourbridge Fair (then held annually just outside of Cambridge and reputed to be the largest fair in Europe), he purchased a glass prism that he found at one of the stalls. Back in his rooms at Trinity College, he noted the rainbow effect of sunlight passing through the prism. Philosophers and scientists had for centuries assumed that sunlight or "white" light was pure and indivisible, but Newton quickly realized that sunlight is a complex of colours which a prism can split up into a spectrum. With further optical improvization, he clinched his point by putting the coloured bands back together again into white light. Thus was born the science of spectroscopy.

But much more was to come from Newton's inventiveness. Labouring under false assumptions about the nature of light, scientists had unsuccessfully attempted to produce a telescope free from blurred images. Newton was by no means content to solve the theoretical problems involved; with his own hands he fashioned in 1668 the world's first reflecting telescope. At last one could get a clear view of the heavens!

Three years later – again with his own hands – he constructed an improved second version, which the Royal Society in London now holds in its vaults as one of its most treasured possessions; and I have been allowed to hold it admiringly in my hands. This little instrument, scarcely over six inches long and with a reflecting mirror only an inch in diameter, has remained for over 250 years the prototype for large reflecting telescopes including the huge ones now in use.

In his pioneering work on the calculus, Newton again demonstrated his flair for both the theoretical and the practical. Once the concept of universal gravitation had leapt into his mind, he was determined to give full expression to his new view of the universe. This task, entailing the writing of his *Principia*, was to occupy him for nearly twenty years; and in the course of it he required a new tool able to deal with dynamic rather than static mathematical entities. The result was that he, along with his contemporary Leibniz (they and their followers quarrelled over the question of priority) invented the differential calculus; this has become an indispensable instrument in practically every branch of engineering as well as in most fields of pure science. Newton also did much to fashion the integral calculus, the tool so widely used for such purposes as finding the areas bounded by curves. One can hardly exaggerate what these practical techniques have meant to world-wide science and engineering down the years since Newton.

The master scientist had his own laboratory in his Trinity College rooms, and during some periods "the fire in the elaboratory scarcely went out." Among other things he experimented with the use of arsenic and antimony in the search for the best alloy for making metal telescope mirrors. He made his own alloys and he himself cast and polished the mirrors.[5]

Newton's irrepressible interest in both the fundamental

and the practical carried him into still other fields. His writings on theology reached the staggering total of some 1,300,000 words, and one of his friends commented that he "was much more solicitous in his inquiries into Religion than into Natural Philosophy."[6] And for many years, as Warden and then Master of the Mint, the great scientist dealt effectively with a wide range of matters affecting the coin of the realm. For many years he also devoted considerable time to alchemy. And as if to prove his undying interest in fundamental physics, he often occupied himself with observing the shape and colour of soap bubbles; and a widow who lived next door to his London home complained that "he diverts himself in the oddest ways imaginable" by sitting with a tub of soap bubbles by his window and blowing bubbles by the hour.[7] Meanwhile, during his long career, Newton was also active in a variety of other capacities including serving as a Member of Parliament and as President of the illustrious Royal Society.[8]

Isaac Newton was *a great interdisciplinarian*, and he dramatically proved the fruitfulness of multidisciplinary approaches. He was a brilliant mathematician and a brilliant physicist, but he was far more besides. He puts to shame the whole over-specialization tendency of recent decades.

Moreover, Newton's life illustrates and dramatizes *the utter practicality of theory*. The pragmatic view of science is shown to be a pathetic one and one that is thoroughly divorced from reality. Science derives its vitality from the continual interaction between theory and application.

Of Newton's successors certainly one of the most illustrious was Sir Humphrey Davy, who revolutionized chemistry. Born in 1778 in Penzance, on the ruggedly beautiful coast of Cornwall, Davy spent his formative years in that area steeped in a folklore of giants, pixies, pirates and smugglers. His father was a talented wood carver of no great ambition, and at first the son distinguished himself by his indolence. His first love seemed to be fishing, a subject on which he later wrote a treatise; indeed fishing preoccupied him throughout his entire scientific career, and just before he died he expressed a last "longing wish to throw a fly."[9]

But as a young boy he was already showing poetic tendencies, and Coleridge was later to remark that Davy would have been the first poet of his age had he not been its first chemist.[10] As Davy himself – writing both as a poet and as a budding scientist – was to express it,

> Oh, most magnificent and noble nature!
> Have I not worshipped thee with such a love
>   As never mortal man before displayed?
> Adored thee in thy majesty of visible creation,
> And searched into thy hidden and mysterious ways
>   As Poet, as Philosopher, as Sage?

Davy also aspired to the medical profession and was apprenticed to a Mr. Porlase, a surgeon-apothecary of Penzance. Meanwhile, on his walks along the cliffs and beaches and on his fishing expeditions, he became impressed with the rich profusion of mineral formations in which the region abounds. He explored the neighbouring tin and copper mines, and he found a good friend in Gregory Watt, whose distinguished father James Watt had recently installed one of his engines to pump water from a nearby mine. Davy found much excitement in visiting the laboratory of a copper works in the vicinity.

Shortly before his twentieth birthday (he was to become a fellow of the Royal Society before he was twenty-five), Davy secured an appointment at something called the Pneumatics Institution, which had been established near Bristol to study the supposedly beneficent influence of various gases on human diseases. Here, among other things, he continued experiments, which he had started in his attic bedroom in Penzance, on the physiological effects of nitrous oxide or "laughing gas." Noting its power to reduce the pain of a toothache which then afflicted him, he anticipated by nearly half a century the first practical use, by an American dentist, of nitrous oxide as an anaesthetic. Davy half killed himself in experiments in which he inhaled various noxious gases, but returning temporarily to Cornwall he quickly recovered with the aid of "luxurious diet and moderate indulgence in wine."

Back in his laboratory, Davy soon started off on a new line of research – the relation of electricity to chemistry – that was to yield momentous results. In Italy, Volta had announced his famous Voltaic pile, the forerunner of modern wet and dry batteries, and had sent a description of it to the Royal Society of London in 1800. Promptly there followed the accidental discovery by British investigators that current from such a pile could decompose water into its constituent oxygen and hydrogen. Fascinated by these finds, Davy leapt into action and in 1801 published six papers on chemical changes achieved by electrolysis. In the same year, Count Rumford, a brilliant scientist, appointed Davy to his recently founded Royal Institution in London.

The Royal Institution had been specifically established to encourage the application of science and invention to the meeting of human needs, and this aim seems to have fitted in well with Davy's conception of science's proper role. His responsibilities included delivering public lectures, and his brilliant discourses on "Chemistry and Its Applications" soon became the rage of London. He plunged into the preparation of other courses of lectures on tanning and on the chemistry of agriculture, and the latter led him into important agricultural research, which he zestfully pursued in proximity to some of his favourite trout streams. Meanwhile, he became superintendent of the Royal Institution.

Davy now embarked on the research that soon made him truly the first scientist of his age. He clearly established the relationship between electrical effects and chemical change, and with marvellous foresight he anticipated large-scale electrolytic decomposition of compounds and the growth of great electrochemical industries such as those of today which annually produce millions of tons of caustic soda from common salt and of aluminium from bauxite. Still more prophetic was Davy's suggestion in 1806 that "however strong the natural electrical energies of bodies may be, yet there is every probability of a limit to their strength: whereas the powers of our artificial instruments seem capable of indefinite increase." This statement might be taken as a vision of the atom-smashing techniques to be developed over a century later.

In a fundamental experiment in 1807, in which he passed a high-voltage electric current through fused caustic soda, Davy for the first time isolated elemental potassium, which burst into flame as soon as it entered the atmosphere. He went on to produce – again for the first time in history – pure magnesium, calcium, strontium, barium, and other elemental substances. He disproved the prevalent notion that hydrochloric acid contains oxygen, and he showed chlorine to be an element in its own right.

But as a token of Davy's depth and breadth of purpose it is significant that full in the middle of his chemical triumphs he seems to have considered entering the church; and he actually put down his name at Cambridge University for studies to qualify himself for the medical profession. In 1810, after he had given a phenomenally successful series of lectures in Ireland, it was stated that he had "given a direction of the public mind towards chemical and philosophical inquiries, which cannot fail . . . to produce the improvement of the sciences, arts and manufactures. . . .'' Three years later, writing to his mother about a forthcoming ''journey of scientific inquiry'' to the Continent, he expressed the hope that it would be ''useful to the world.''

In 1814, Davy showed that iodine is an elemental substance and gave it its present name. Using a large burning-glass, he pioneered in the combustion of diamonds; he proved that they were made of carbon, and in so doing he helped to demolish the accepted theory that bodies alike in composition must show some resemblance in form. He studied coal gas and prophesied its future economic value.

Following a coal mine disaster in 1812, he applied his knowledge of pure science to designing the famous Davy safety lamp. He wrote to his sponsors that it ''will give me great satisfaction if my chemical knowledge can be of any use in an enquiry so interesting to humanity''; and in a matter of weeks he had discovered the principle that incipient explosions of firedamp (methane) cannot be communicated through small apertures such as those of a fine-mesh screen. After he had designed an effective safety lamp he reported to his sponsors that ''I have never received so much pleasure from the result of any of my chemical labours; for I trust the cause of humanity will gain something by it.''

It is part of Davy's genius that he launched Michael Faraday (1791–1867) on his career. Faraday was like Newton and Davy in having compulsive multidisciplinary tendencies. As John Meurig Thomas, Faraday's biographer, has expressed it, ''His rich imagination pertained to things other than the scientific. . . . The beauty of nature, . . . especially the hills of Devonshire, the vales of South Wales, all . . . landscapes and the seascapes of Brighton or the Isle of Wight, could move him to lyrical ecstasy. . . .''[11]

The story is well known of how young Faraday, a bookbinder's apprentice, came to some of Davy's lectures and was so enthralled by them that he summarized them in his copperplate handwriting, bound the product in leather, and sent it to the great man with a plea to become his assistant. Davy became intrigued with what a lesser person might have regarded as an impertinence, and when an opportunity arose gave Faraday just what he had asked for.

Even as a young apprentice, Faraday had set up his own small laboratory in his room over the bindery. (Later he was to write a detailed manual on laboratory management.) Many books passed through the bindery, and it was in a volume of the *Encyclopaedia Britannica*, in an article on the work of such men as Galvani and Volta, that he had first met electricity. With his own hands he had made various electrical machines, including one with a crank turning a glass cylinder which rubbed against a piece of velvet and gradually charged it with static electricity; it was a crude version of the later Helmholtz electrostatic machine. He had also performed a variety of chemical experiments.

Soon after his appointment in 1813 to the Royal Institution, Faraday set off with Davy on a two-year scientific tour of the Continent. During the tour, they made observations on everything from electric eels to volcanoes, performed numerous experiments, and met leading chemists and some of the pioneers in electricity. In 1816, Faraday published his first paper, on the analysis of caustic lime he had found in Tuscany. His output increased to six scientific papers in 1817 and eleven in 1818. Already he was well launched on what was to become a career of science and public service.

His first major achievement came soon thereafter. In 1820 the Danish scientist Hans Christian Oersted had by chance discovered a relation between magnetism and electricity; when he had moved a wire connected to a battery over a compass needle, the needle had deflected. Oersted had promptly published a paper on the phenomenon, and this had set off an international electricity race, in which both Davy and Faraday enthusiastically joined. In 1821, Faraday constructed the world's first electric motor – an historic breakthrough.

Its design was simplicity itself. Using wax as an adhesive, Faraday planted a straight bar magnet in a vertical position in the bottom of a bowl. He then poured mercury into the bowl until only the top of the bar magnet protruded. One wire from a battery he ran into the mercury, and the other wire he stuck into a cork which floated on the mercury's surface. As the current flowed, the cork went round and round the bar magnet in the manner of a small boat circling a buoy. All subsequent electric motors have relied on this same principle of a rotor revolving within a magnetic field; nowadays, of course, the rotor generally turns on its own axle within the field, but the concept remains the same.

Faraday's achievements in electricity had only begun, but he now shifted his attention to alloy steels. With a collaborator named Stodart, who died while the two-year project was in progress, he prepared the first stainless steels. Here Faraday collided with an obstacle that he was to encounter over and over during his long career: conservatism and lack of imagination on the part of industry. By not taking advantage of the new stainless steels, the manufacturers missed a great opportunity.

Although it later developed that another investigator had antedated him, Faraday liquefied chlorine in 1823. He thus helped lay the basis for the modern refrigeration industry, which is founded on the principle that as liquefied gases return to the gaseous state they absorb heat from their surroundings. Two years later, in a further demonstration of multidisciplinary prowess, he pioneered in discovering benzene. This discovery ranked as Faraday's greatest achievement in the field of chemistry, and it provided a foundation for the great organic chemical industry of today.

In 1824 Faraday was appointed for life to a new chair of chemistry at the Royal Institution, but his interests lay even more in physics. In 1831 came the great breakthrough. He discovered the principle that currents could be generated by electromagnetic means. William Sturgeon, an Englishman, and Joseph Henry, an American, had already made electromagnets, and one of Henry's could lift 650 pounds; but Faraday was about to take still more important steps. After many experiments, he found that if a current from a battery were passed through a coil wound around one side of an iron ring, it would induce a current in a similar coil on the opposite side; this was to provide the basis for all future transformers.

Then Faraday found that if he wound many turns of wire around a hollow paper cylinder and thrust a bar magnet into the cylinder, a current would flow in the coil. He had now, for the first time in history, converted mechanical motion into a current of electricity. Not surprisingly, it has been said that modern civilization owes more to the principle of electromagnetic induction than to any other single scientific concept.

But Faraday was not content merely to discover the principle. In tending batteries at the Royal Institution, he had become impressed with how heavy and cumbersome they were, and he now conceived the idea of producing electricity by simpler means. Moving the bar magnet inside the paper cylinder had given only a sporadic current, but he was intent upon generating a useful steady one, and later in that same year he succeeded. Having already made the world's first electric motor, he now constructed the world's first electric dynamo, which again was beautiful in its simplicity.

Faraday mounted a copper disk on a copper axle

equipped with a crank. The disk was set between the two poles of a horseshoe magnet which was especially designed so that its poles would almost touch the disk. A wire ran from a galvanometer to the axle, and a second wire from the galvanometer was in contact with the disk's outer edge. When the crank was turned, the galvanometer showed a continuing deflection. Although much work remained to be done to improve the design of dynamos and increase their capacity, this achievement paved the way for all future mechanical electric generators, including those in the enormous nuclear and conventional power stations of today.

For thirty years after the 1831 breakthrough, with only occasional lapses, Faraday pushed his researches in electricity and magnetism, and his thousands of patient experiments yielded many another important find. For example, his analysis of magnetic lines of force foreshadowed the work of Maxwell, Einstein, and others, and showed the way for all future designers of electrical machinery. Faraday demonstrated the homogeneity of electricity produced by friction, batteries, dynamos, and various other means, and he concluded that "Electricity, whatever its source, is identical in its nature."

Faraday coined such terms as "electrode," "anode," "cathode," and "electrolysis"; and he showed how to use electrolytic methods to measure quantities of electricity. By successfully twisting a beam of polarized light with a magnet, he pointed scientific thought towards the electromagnetic theory of light. He proved that flames and gases respond to magnetic influence, and his far-reaching mind discerned hints of subatomic particles, such as electrons, which were to be discovered many years later. In addition he found time, in interdisciplinary fashion, to delve into many other subjects; for instance, in a paper on what he termed "optical deception," he helped to lay the basis for the modern motion-picture and television industries by elucidating what happens when the eye gets a rapid succession of glimpses of a moving body.

Faraday also did a great deal of consulting work. An especially fruitful consulting relationship was with Trinity House, the body responsible for England's lighthouses, to which he became scientific adviser in 1836 and which he served for many years. Many seamen owed their lives to Faraday's application of the magnetoelectric spark to lighthouse illumination. Referring to his work on behalf of mariners, he once observed that there is "no part of my life which gives me more delight."

During his long life, Faraday prepared an incredible range of reports and recommendations on the most amazing variety of subjects. Here are a few samples: building arches; preventing dry rot in timber; ventilating the House of Lords; preserving stonework in the face of Britain's climate; installing lightning rods on structures; making pencils and steel and quill pens; analysing paper and manufacturing envelopes by machine; silvering mirrors; compensating compasses on board iron ships; protecting the ships from corrosion by sea water; illuminating art galleries by gaslight; tunnelling under the Thames; preventing mine and boiler explosions; wearing asbestos suits for rescue work; maintaining the strength of good English ale; and magnetically locating pieces of metal requiring surgical removal. And through all of this there ran the unifying theme of science in the service of man.

Equally impressed with the constructive practical potentialities of basic science was Louis Pasteur (1822–95). In a way, his theoretical work harks back to that of Davy; for just as Davy brilliantly elucidated the relationship between chemistry and electricity, so Pasteur did the same for chemis-

try and biology. Like Davy and Faraday, Pasteur, whose
father was a tanner, rose from humble origins.

Pasteur was born in Dole, an ancient French city not far
from the Swiss border, but spent most of his childhood and
attended school in the nearby town of Arbois. His father
instilled in his son a fierce love for France and all she stood
for and both father and son received the red ribbon of the
Legion of Honour: the one for valorously serving his country
in Napoleon's armies, the other for no less patriotic contributions such as were to make him France's greatest-ever
scientist.

Pasteur also resembled Davy in that as a young boy he
was a mediocre student; and his flair for the fine arts also
reminds one of Davy's talent in poetry. He early showed
ability in both singing and painting; but gradually his interests turned to chemistry, and his last painting, a sensitive
portrait of his father, was completed when he was nineteen.

Already determined to qualify himself as a university professor in chemistry, Pasteur continued his studies in Paris.
In 1847, at the age of 25, he completed all requirements
for the Doctor of Science degree at the École Normale,
France's foremost training ground for teachers; and meanwhile he had obtained a job there as assistant to Professor
Barlard, a leading chemist.

Just as had Faraday before him when he became Davy's
assistant, Pasteur found ample incentive to push original
research. In keeping with the Frenchman's interest in anything concerning wine, Pasteur decided to investigate tartaric acid, which many years earlier had been isolated from
the hard crusty deposits found in wine barrels. Chemical
manufacturers had learned to make tartaric acid in quantity
for medicinal and other purposes; but one manufacturer
had accidentally produced a substance that seemed similar
to, yet unaccountably different from, tartaric acid. The great

French chemist Gay-Lussac had named this racemic acid, in honour of the grape (in Latin *racemus*); but nobody knew just what it was or its relation to ordinary tartaric acid.

Pasteur was determined to find out. In the spirit of Isaac Newton he had already learned glass-blowing, carpentry, and metalworking; and now with his own hands he constructed a polarimeter with which he could pass a beam of polarized light through solutions of various crystals and observe whether and to what extent they rotated the beam. There was nothing new about the instrument itself, but there was in the use Pasteur made of it; for in a brilliant piece of scientific detective work he showed that by their crystalline structures one could infallibly distinguish between tartaric and racemic acids. With this discovery, which created a stir in scientific circles, Pasteur acquired a reputation almost overnight. His work heralded the modern science of stereo-chemistry, which studies the molecular architecture of crystals; also it was to lead indirectly to his momentous investigation of fermentation and in turn to the germ theory of disease.

In 1848, Pasteur became assistant professor of chemistry at the University of Strasbourg, and in the following year he married a daughter of one of the university's administrative officers. Continuing his studies of crystals, he enhanced France's already high position in this field, which she still retains. In 1852 he was promoted to full professor and a few months later he joined his father in the Legion of Honour.

But during all those years, Pasteur could not overcome his fascination with racemic acid. On a field tour of factories producing tartaric acid, he had found that racemic acid remained in the mother liquor after the main product had crystallized out, but he had failed in all attempts to make the stuff in his laboratory. Realizing that racemic acid should have many practical uses, the Pharmaceutical Society of Paris in 1853 offered a prize to him who should first synthesize it. After prodigious effort Pasteur won the award, and to his father back in the old tannery he wrote, "This discovery will have incalculable consequences."

This unfounded, intuitive prediction proved to be no exaggeration. Already Pasteur's imagination had conjured up an analogy between chemistry and life. As he watched his crystals growing and developing from the mother liquor which gave them birth, he noted that broken crystals, like injured tissues in the body, heal and are typically restored to their original form.

But the big breakthrough followed an accident – one of those happy accidents which, as Pasteur always insisted, favour "the prepared mind." One day in his laboratory he noticed that a tartaric acid solution had become contaminated by a green mould. Instead of fretfully discarding the solution, he let it stimulate his imagination.

Previously, he had found that although a solution of tartaric acid rotated the beam of light in his polarimeter, normal racemic acid was optically inactive because half its molecules tended to rotate the beam one way while the other half exerted an opposite tendency. Would a mouldy solution of racemic acid behave in the same way? Pasteur tried it and the result electrified him. The solution had become optically active and he immediately understood why. Feeding selectively upon one kind of molecule in preference to the other, the yeast had caused a *chemical* change in the racemic acid.

Pasteur's imagination having led him into an uncharted realm, his practical bent now grasped the implications: microbes could *deliberately* be employed to bring about desired chemical changes. He was in due course to apply this principle in ways that carried the most momentous effects for industry, agriculture, medicine, and in turn for science.

In 1854, Pasteur was appointed professor of chemistry and dean at the new Faculty of Sciences in the industrial city of Lille in northern France. A lesser man would have balked at cutting himself off from the established centres of unsullied science and academic respectability, but in Lille's comparatively prosaic atmosphere Pasteur found just the challenge he needed to achieve a harmonious mating of theory and practice.

The cares of industry soon spurred him to a major conceptual advance. A local alcohol factory, owned by the father of one of his students, was encountering inexplicable difficulties in the fermentation of sugar beet. At that time, since nobody in science or industry knew the real nature of fermentation, no one could explain why the mash often went sour. Pasteur almost literally immersed himself in the problem; as his wife wrote, "Louis is now up to his neck in beet juice." He soon found that every good batch of mash was overrun with yeast cells but every bad one contained millions of another kind of microbe which he identified as lactic acid. He postulated that both kinds of microbes were living things; as the yeast fed upon beet sugar it gave off alcohol, while from the same food the interloping bacilli produced lactic acid with its souring effect. He showed how the factory could employ simple microscopic techniques to control the quality of its output.

But this was only the beginning of Pasteur's rendezvous with beet juice, for it led straight to his revolutionary paper of 1857 entitled "A Memoir on Fermentation Called Lactic." Flying full in the face of all respectable dogma, his paper gave the world's first clear formulation of the germ theory of fermentation; and by that very token it revolutionized much of industry and medicine.

In the same year, Pasteur returned to Paris to become administrator and director of scientific studies at his old

École Normale, where he could better develop his germ theory and combat the widespread opposition to it. He also became professor of organic chemistry at the Sorbonne. His adversaries were both numerous and prestigious, and an interesting feature of his career is that he was twice defeated for admission to the French Academy of Sciences before that august body finally relented, and that later the Academy of Medicine admitted this scientific revolutionary by a margin of one vote.

For many years Pasteur's opponents, seeking to refute his view that microbes multiply by reproduction, argued that to the contrary they spontaneously come to life out of dead matter. But gradually he beat back or converted those who disbelieved him; and by 1864, when he summarized his experiments in a brilliant lecture at the Sorbonne, the battle had been conclusively won. Throughout it, Pasteur had never claimed that spontaneous generation of life was theoretically impossible; he merely insisted that under no known circumstances "can we affirm that microscopic beings come into the world without germs, without parents of their own nature."

Both Pasteur and his adversaries were at that time unaware of the biological quirk whereby some microbes form spores which can remain inactive for long periods and may even resist the temperature of boiling water. When this fact came to light a few years later, Pasteur invented the autoclave, the sterilizing device still in general use today. Generating superheated steam under pressure, it can kill even the most persistent spores.

During this period, the French wine industry was suffering because the product so often became sour or bitter or "ropy," and Pasteur was asked to solve yet another theoretical/practical problem. He was now led to discover the principle of halting or retarding the growth of undesirable microbes by partial heat sterilization or pasteurization as it soon came to be called, and of course the process now finds worldwide use for safeguarding milk and other foodstuffs. Having evolved the theory, Pasteur went on to design practical industrial equipment to implement it.

In 1865, a delegation of senators from the south of France came to Pasteur and implored him to investigate a mysterious disease (or pair of diseases as it turned out) which was ruining the raw silk industry of their region. When Pasteur objected that he had no specialist knowledge whatever about silk culture or the silk industry, the head of the delegation wisely replied, "Dr. Pasteur, that is exactly why we have come to you."

The result was decisive – both for the industry and for science and medicine. This five-year project was to give Pasteur his first opportunity *to extend his germ theory to diseases of animals and man*; in effect his first patients were silkworms. In the midst of it he suffered the stroke which was to leave him partially paralyzed for the rest of his life. But this did not stop him; he devised control measures which saved the industry and which he incorporated into a two-volume treatise on silkworm culture.

Meanwhile Joseph Lister, the great British surgeon, had become the first to apply Pasteur's germ theory in medical practice. Appalled by the number of surgical patients who died from gangrene and blood poisoning, he transferred Pasteur's ideas to the development of antiseptic surgical techniques, including the use of a carbolic acid spray which disinfected the air in the operating room. Deaths from postoperative infection dramatically diminished, but years were to elapse and thousands of lives were to be needlessly wasted before Lister could secure general acceptance of his methods. It testifies to his stature that Lister gave Pasteur complete and unqualified credit "for having by your brilliant researches demonstrated the truth of the germ theory of putrefaction and thus furnished me with the principle upon which alone the antiseptic system can be carried out."

Having vindicated his germ theory with respect to higher animals, Pasteur now dreamed of its humanitarian application in the actual prevention of disease. Again a happy accident supervened. In 1879, when he was studying chicken cholera, he went to spend the summer in his native Arbois. Before leaving Paris, he instructed his assistants to tend the cholera cultures by regularly transplanting them to fresh nutrient media; but the assistants departed on a brief holiday and failed in their duty. Returning from their holiday, the assistants in routine fashion injected chickens with some of the cholera culture; to their astonishment, the chickens lived and even continued healthy when they were subsequently injected with a freshly prepared and obviously lethal culture.

The moment Pasteur heard the news he was overcome with excitement; for instantly he realized that the chickens had been immunized or vaccinated. (Edward Jenner, the English physician, had many years earlier invented vaccination for smallpox; but nobody knew why the method succeeded and nobody had been able to apply the principle to any other disease.) After months of furious labour, Pasteur perfected all the techniques needed for the large-scale immunization of chickens with cultures of weakened cholera microbes; and these methods find use throughout the world today.

Against the opposition of many veterinary surgeons who felt that he was unqualified in their field, Pasteur now turned to anthrax; and before long he had developed a vaccine to control it. In a sensational public demonstration before farmers and veterinarians, he proved the merit of his vaccine by injecting virulent anthrax microbes into a large number of immunized and non-immunized sheep and other animals; all those animals which had been immunized lived, and all the others died.

Pasteur went on to develop a rabies vaccine that could prevent the disease in dogs even after they had been bitten by rabid animals. Then in 1885, just as he was wondering if he should try the vaccine on himself after deliberately contracting the disease, there was brought to him a young boy who had been savagely attacked by a mad dog. There seemed no choice but to vaccinate, and the boy's life was spared. Pasteur personally saved the lives of hundreds of other rabies victims, and his discoveries led to immunization techniques against further diseases caused both by microbes and by viruses such as those responsible for yellow fever and polio.

The venerable gentleman, who ever since his stroke had walked with a limp, and whose theories countless monodisciplinary experts had condemned, died peacefully just before the end of the new century which he had already helped to shape. His place was secure.

Pasteur was passionately devoted to his work and, linked with that, he was a bold and enormously successful multidisciplinarian. As Anthony Daniels points out in his review of Patrice Debre's monumental biography of Pasteur, "There is scarcely anyone alive today without reason to be grateful to Pasteur, and there are very few figures in history of whom that may be said."[12]

We have now briefly surveyed the achievements of four of history's greatest multidisciplinary scientists. Their intellectual legacy we shall in this book designate as *Scientific Idealism.* This connects with the tradition of philosophical idealism which goes back even to Plato and his antecedents.

But before elucidating the full significance of Scientific

Idealism, it is well to gain perspective by considering the very different point of view of that great thinker Karl Marx with his so-called Scientific Socialism. To this we now turn.

IV The Great Experiment

Among definitive recent histories of latter-day Russia are Orlando Figes's *A People's Tragedy*, running to over 900 pages; Robert Service's *A History of Twentieth-Century Russia*, with some 650 pages; and *Russia: A History*, edited by Gregory L. Freeze, with just under 500 pages.[1] The purpose of the present chapter is briefly to highlight certain aspects of Russia's history which are pertinent to our overall theme.

Karl Marx profoundly influenced Russia – and the world at large. According to an official Soviet-era biography of Marx, "The most advanced, scientific world outlook, which has given mankind and the proletariat, its most advanced revolutionary class, a great instrument for cognising and changing the world, was developed by and named after Marx."[2] As the biography further explains, "It was he who turned socialism from a utopia into a science and provided a profound theoretical explanation for the inevitable downfall of capitalism and the triumph of socialism."[3]

Scholars throughout the world recognize Karl Heinrich Marx (1818–83) as one of the truly great thinkers of the nineteenth century; indeed, taking the longer view "he owned one of the mighty minds of the human race," as Clinton Rossiter has put it. Marx drastically altered every branch of social thinking, which has continued to bear his imprint ever since. Moreover, part of Marx's genius lay in his insistence that it is not enough to understand the world; the main point is to change it. Terry Eagleton writes of Marx's "special kind of action-oriented theory."[4]

Marx's insistence on action was prophetic, and his wishes were to be fulfilled – but not in the way he had anticipated. He had thought that his revolution would begin in Britain as the most advanced industrial nation of the day; but instead it took place in a vast country extending over eleven time zones as against, for example, five time zones for the mainland United States. Russia, then, was to be the scene of the Great Marxist Experiment.

And how can we best define the Marxist system? One definition identifies it as "The philosophical system, also known as dialectical materialism or scientific Socialism, founded by Marx and Engels."[5] This definition has the great advantage of emphasizing the philosophy-focused nature of the system.

Perhaps the most useful of all, however, is the following definition from the *International Encyclopedia of the Social Sciences*:

> Marxism is a dialectical theory of human progress. It regards history as the development of man's efforts to master the forces of nature, and hence, of production. . . . Since all production is carried out within social organization, history is the succession of changes in social systems, the development of human relations geared to productive activity . . . , in which the economic system forms the 'base' and all other relationships, institutions, and idea systems are superstructural.[6]

If Marxism developed a body of theory, equally it emphasized practice. This was of course especially dramatized by *The Communist Manifesto*, as written jointly by Marx and his collaborator and benefactor Friedrich Engels (1820–95) and published in 1848. In the view of Marx and Engels, the capitalist bourgeoisie "cannot exist without constantly revolutionizing the instruments of production, and . . . the whole relations of society." Crediting it with astonishing feats, they declared that the bourgeoisie,

> during its rule of scarce one hundred years, has created more massive and more colossal productive forces than all preceding generations together. Subjection of Nature's forces to man, machinery, application of chemistry to industry and agriculture, steam-navigation, railways, electric telegraphs, clearing of whole continents for cultivation, canalization of rivers, whole populations conjured out of the ground – what earlier century had even a presentiment that such productive forces slumbered in the lap of social labour?[7]

But the bourgeoisie's very success, claimed Marx and Engels, would prove its undoing. "The productive forces at the disposal of society no longer tend to further the conditions of bourgeois property; on the contrary, they have become too powerful for those conditions. . . ." And again, "not only has the bourgeoisie forged the weapons that bring death to itself; it has also called into existence the men who are to wield those weapons – the modern working class – the proletarians."

Now it is of course well known that Marx laid great stress upon the notion of class and the class struggle; in the *Manifesto*, for example, he and Engels gave pride of place to the declaration that "The history of all hitherto existing society . . . is the history of class struggles." This enabled them to develop the argument leading up to the famous call to action which supplied the *Manifesto's* climax: "WORKING MEN OF ALL COUNTRIES, UNITE!"[8]

The story of how Russia became the world's first major Marxist state is a fascinating one and one full of pathos. Of the many factors involved, certainly a crucial one related to the role of Germany and of German psychological warfare. As Edward Jay Epstein points out,

> The word 'disinformation' was in fact coined by the German High Command (OKW) during World War I. . . . Whereas deception had always been part of German military tactics at the field level, the development of the radio forced these tactical deceptions to be centrally co-ordinated. The OKW thus set up a special unit, called the Disinformation Service, to co-ordinate the forged radio traffic that was likely to be intercepted by British, French and Russian intelligence. . . .[9]

After having proved their effectiveness, especially in disrupting the war effort against Germany, the German deception staff in April 1917 launched what Epstein rightly calls one of the most successful pieces of planned subversion in modern history. German military intelligence arranged a special sealed train which took the Marxist revolutionary V. I. Lenin (1870–1924) and his accomplices from Switzerland, where they had been in exile, to the Russian border, where they were smuggled in and immediately began to disrupt the Russian war effort. Within a year, Lenin had seized supreme power, and this led inexorably to the creation in 1922 of the Union of Soviet Socialist Republics or Soviet Union.

From the German point of view, here was a brilliant strategy which soon removed the need for Germany's armies to fight simultaneously on two major fronts. From the Russian point of view it was a disaster.

As Figes points out in his monumental *A People's Tragedy*, "The Russian Revolution was, at least in terms of its effects, one of the biggest events in the history of the world."[10] Russia would never be the same again and the world would never be the same again.

Roland W. Clark, in his definitive biography of Lenin,[11] has with great care and objectively uncovered that leader's thinking and his performance. It was in 1918, for example, that Lenin established the Extraordinary Commission for Combatting Counter-Revolution, Speculation and Sabotage – i.e., the Cheka secret police – which quickly developed into "the country's most feared organization." Lenin then used the Cheka to suppress all political parties apart from his own.[12]

Especially after an attack on Lenin's life in August 1918, there followed "a dramatic increase in the activities of the Cheka, which even during the preceding months had steadily been transforming isolated executions into a widespread and organized campaign soon rightly known as the Red Terror." As for Lenin's personal involvement, "There can be no doubt about his knowledge and encouragement of the killings which took place by the thousands from the summer of 1918 onwards."[13]

As Clark reminds us, terror "had a long ancestry in Russia, and from the mid-nineteenth century onwards both the Tsarist authorities and many revolutionary groups used it in efforts to achieve their ends...."[14] But Lenin and his dreaded Cheka extended and systemized the process more than was ever done by the nineteenth or twentieth century Tsars.

As Robert Conquest points out, Lenin had developed a theoretical justification for terror as early as 1905. Moreover, he "continually insisted on intensified terror against the judgement of many of his subordinates." Lenin never forgot the theoretical – i.e., Marxist – rationale for terror. Thus in 1918, after alluding to the misgivings even among hardened

Bolsheviks at the extremes of the Cheka, Lenin stated:

> When we are reproached with cruelty, we wonder how people can forget the most elementary Marxism. . . . The most important thing for us to remember is that the Cheka is directly carrying out the dictatorship of the proletariat, and in this respect its services are invaluable.[15]

It is in this sense that Lenin's was a policy of cold *calculated* mass terror. With Lenin, Marx's "scientific socialism" provided a proper basis for what Clark has termed the "unqualified ruthlessness with which he was prepared to pursue his aims in the sacred cause of the Revolution." And he quotes a contemporary observer who referred to Lenin's "abstract social hatred and cold political cruelty."[16]

For good reason Stalin is regarded as a tyrant, but many people fail to appreciate that Lenin provided the complete groundwork for Stalin's behaviour. People often forget that *it was Lenin, not Stalin*, who inaugurated the Red Terror which flourished from early in the life of the new Soviet state. Moreover, it was *Lenin, not Stalin*, who first instituted the bizarre "show trials," leading to certain execution of the accused, which later became so characteristic of Stalin's rule.[17]

While Lenin was consolidating his totalitarian power within the Soviet Union, he had not forgotten about the German connection. He had received substantial German help, both in money and in intelligence, in consummating his coup. Moreover, he was not slow to learn the disinformation and deception techniques employed by the Germans. Although Germany's Disinformation Service was officially disbanded after World War I, its officers and its methods played a major role in mounting a gigantic subterfuge, code-named "Operation Kama," which paradoxically took place mainly in the Soviet Union and with Lenin's connivance. Designed to evade the arms prohibitions in the Versailles Treaty, the programme, as secretly agreed by Lenin and continued until 1933, included the construction of German munitions plants and training facilities in the Soviet Union in exchange for German industrial equipment and patents.[18] Thus Lenin was unwittingly helping to pave the way for the rise of Hitler and his dictatorship and also for the notorious later agreement between Hitler and Stalin.

Hitler's own deception planners adopted a chilling technique to help bring about that agreement. Knowing that Stalin was paranoid about possible plots to overthrow him, they arranged to feed the Soviet security services with credible disinformation which would persuade Stalin that there was indeed such a conspiracy.[19] This was one of the factors which led Stalin to launch his massive purge of the Soviet armed forces. As Anthony Read and David Fisher point out in their carefully-researched book *The Deadly Embrace,*

> . . . most reliable estimates place the number of men who were either shot or sent to labour camps at around 35,000. At least half of the army's entire officer strength was removed, including three out of five marshals, thirteen out of fifteen army commanders, 220 out of 406 brigade commanders, seventy-five of the eighty members of the supreme military council, including every single commander of a military district, and all eleven vice-commissars of war. The remnants were inexperienced, disorganized and completely demoralized, and the modernization programmes, which had been progressing well, were utterly shattered.[20]

Earlier, in his so-called Testament written shortly before his death, Lenin had expressed some doubts as to whether Stalin would be the proper person to succeed him. Lenin need not have worried. Having constructed a totalitarian system and having ruthlessly presided over the growth of the Soviet police state, Lenin was almost bound to be followed by a leader who was equally ruthless if not more so. Lenin, as Clark suggests, "paved the way first for the enormities of the Cheka and then for the even greater enormities perpetrated by Stalin."[21]

In the opinion of Lenin, and of his successor Stalin, any successful farmer, or any successful business man, was by definition an enemy of the people and was to be dealt with accordingly. Many millions of such people, together with their families, were either slaughtered on the spot or exiled to labour camps, where more often than not they died of hunger, exposure and exhaustion. (I have Russian friends whose families were decimated in this way.) The authorities particularly reserved their venom for the kulaks, a catch-all term including independent farmers and others as convenient. As Stalin was to put it, "We must smash the kulaks, eliminate them as a class."[22]

Famine was of course not unknown in pre-Soviet Russia; and a prime example was the famine of 1891–92 when the rains failed and dust-bowl conditions were created over large areas of the country. Many voluntary organizations emerged to help people provide famine relief, and ironically the Marxists seized the opportunity to spread their creed among them.[23]

Such famines were *natural* disasters; but on the other hand Lenin and Stalin created massive *man-made* famine disasters – especially through excessive requisitioning of grain from the independent farmers and through forcing them to join collective farms. As Moynahan has expressed it,

Collectivization was a social and economic disaster. Communist ideology, honed in the reading rooms of Western Europe, broke the spirit of the villages and turned the fields barren.

Grain production slumped disastrously. Peasants forced to join collectives on pain of deportation to the Siberian wastes would sign up in the morning and then in the evening would slaughter their livestock, smash machines and destroy crops rather than let the State have them. They gorged themselves on the slaughtered animals so that 'everyone had a greasy mouth . . . everyone blinked like an owl, as if drunk from eating.' Slaughter was present even if it brought starvation. Three years after the start of collectivization, the number of sheep and goats was reduced by two-thirds, of horses by half, of cattle by nearly half. Because communism is so clearly the work of intellectuals, because its ideology appears, like the language, so complex; because it ruled so much of the earth – it is difficult to dismiss it as one would, say, a quack medicine. But collectivization was no more than the act of simpletons and sadists.[24]

Particularly acute was the famine of 1921–22, when many millions of Russians died of starvation and cannibalism was not unknown. At that time my father was an assistant to Herbert Hoover, who was of course to become US President immediately before Franklin D. Roosevelt. Hoover had created the American Relief Administration to supply food and medicines to post-war Europe.

A group of public-spirited Russians wrote to Hoover to appeal for aid for their famine-stricken country, and Hoover responded positively. Lenin was furious, for he had decreed that officially the famine did not exist. He had his secret police arrest the public-spirited citizens on spurious charges and most of them were sent into exile.

But it was too late for Lenin to refuse Hoover's public offer of aid, and so a team including my father arrived in the then Soviet Union. On behalf of ARA – as Russians affectionately called it – my father travelled far and wide in that vast country. Often he would visit villages aboard a traditional three-horse Russian troika. Sometimes hungry wolves would pursue the troika, and that was a bit disconcerting.

From my earliest childhood my father used to tell me of his experiences in what became almost his adopted homeland. He used to speak of his love for the ordinary Russian people, who kept their sense of humour despite all adversities. "What marvellous people and what a miserable system," my father used to say.

By the autumn of 1922, when its activities were at their height, ARA was feeding *ten million Russians every day*. ARA also, as Figes points out, dispatched great quantities of medicines, clothing, tools and seed – the seed "enabling the two successive bumper harvests of 1922 and 1923 that finally secured Russia's recovery from the famine."[25]

Meanwhile the American public were horrified to learn that, during the very height of Russia's famine, Lenin was busy *exporting* large quantities of food to earn hard currency for his own pet projects. But before ARA's Russian programme was terminated in mid-1923, Maxim Gorky, one of the public-spirited citizens who had been ostracized by Lenin, wrote to Herbert Hoover as follows:

In all the history of human suffering I know of nothing more trying to the souls of men than the events through which the Russian people are passing, and in the history of practical humanitarianism I know of no accomplishment which in terms of magnitude and generosity can be compared to the relief that you have actually accomplished. Your help will enter history as a unique gigantic achievement, worthy of the greatest glory, which will long remain in the memory of millions of Russians whom you have saved from death. The generosity of the American people resuscitates the dream of fraternity among people at a time when humanity greatly needs charity and compassion.[26]

Meanwhile, faced with ever-growing opposition to his regime, Lenin had come to fear that it might not survive. In 1921 – as a purely tactical U-turn – he decided temporarily to reinstate private enterprise in industry, trade, and agriculture. Thus was born his so-called New Economic Policy or NEP. As Winston Churchill wrote of Lenin's introduction of the NEP, "He repudiated what he had slaughtered so many for not believing. They were right it seemed after all. They were unlucky in that he did not find it out before."[27]

And of course the New Economic Policy was not to last, for under Stalin the surviving kulaks were to be brutally dispossessed and collectivized in a wholesale return to "sound" Marxist principles. And of course the whole of the Soviet economy was to be subjected to those same principles.

But while it did last, the New Economic Policy achieved remarkable things. In a way it seemed like a caricature of capitalism. Many so-called Nepmen – especially among the traders and industrialists – grew rich. They bedecked their women in expensive jewelry and they adopted a lavish lifestyle. This in turn provoked much popular resentment.

While it lasted, the NEP indeed registered astonishing results. As Service has expressed it,

> Economically it appeared that the NEP had succeeded beyond everyone's expectations. . . . By 1923, cereal production had increased by twenty-three percent over the total recorded for 1920. Domestic industrial recovery also gathered pace: in the same three years output from the factories rose by 184 percent. . . .[28]

It was not long before Lenin's death in 1924 that, as already indicated, he used his famous Testament to express doubts about Stalin as his anointed successor. He even went on to suggest "that the comrades think of a way of removing

Stalin from that post" as Secretary-General of the Communist Party.[29] But of course that was not to be, and Stalin quickly consolidated his absolute power.

Lenin, having constructed a totalitarian system, and having ruthlessly presided over the growth of the Soviet police state, was almost bound to be followed by a leader who was equally ruthless if not more so. It is worth repeating Clark's statement that Lenin paved the way for a tyrant like Stalin and for Stalin's even greater enormities.[30]

Under Stalin the NEP was abolished and there was mass collectivization of agriculture including the slaughter or deportation of most of the remaining kulaks and their families with consequent widespread famine.

Meanwhile, in 1928, Stalin launched the first of a series of rigid five-year plans which consolidated his grip over the entire Soviet society and every citizen in it. Under Stalin, the slightest show of dissent would lead inexorably to prison or much worse.

Then came the horrors of the Second World War – when, for example, more than one million Russian citizens died in the Nazi siege of Leningrad (later renamed St.Petersburg) – followed by the allied victory and Stalin's consolidation of his empire.

In terms of human rights, progress within the Soviet Union was excruciatingly slow. Stalin died in 1953, and three years later, Nikita S. Khrushchev, in a secret speech, denounced Stalin for his tyrannical rule. In spite of Khrushchev's courage, the Soviet Union remained a police state; but dissent could not be stifled forever.

It was Stalin, who for all his sins, had initiated the so-called policy of peaceful coexistence, and he did this for several compelling reasons including the West's initial nuclear supremacy, the growing moral authority of the United Nations, the Truman Doctrine, the creation of NATO, the

success of the Berlin airlift, and the military response of the
United Nations in Korea. Stalin hoped that he had found
in the concept a new kind of weapon.

Khrushchev, while castigating the author of the concept,
nevertheless eagerly embraced it as if it were his own. But
at the same time he condemned those who tried to extend
peaceful coexistence into the *ideological* sphere. At the Twentieth Congress of the Communist Party of the Soviet Union,
in 1956, Krushchev declared:

> It does not follow at all from the fact that we stand for peaceful
> coexistence and economic competition with capitalism that the
> struggle against bourgeois ideology, against bourgeois survivals,
> can be relaxed. Our task is tirelessly to expose bourgeois ideol-
> ogy, reveal how inimical it is to people, and show up its reaction-
> ary nature.[31]

He subsequently explained that ideological coexistence
would not become possible until Communism was everywhere triumphant, and referring to the so-called capitalist
world he declared, "We will bury you!"

Krushchev presided over the Soviet invasion of Hungary
and the building of the Berlin Wall; and it was he who
brought the world to the brink of nuclear war in the Cuban
missile crisis of 1962. Meanwhile the Soviet economy was
stagnating. In 1964 Khruschev abruptly fell from power; and
two days after his dismissal *Pravda* denounced his "hare-
brained scheming, immature conclusions, hasty decisions,
and actions divorced from reality."

Subsequently several successive Soviet heads of state
briefly held power; and meanwhile the ideological vacuum
had become acute. For helping to fill that vacuum the world
is indeed indebted to, among others, two great Russian dissidents: Alexander Solzhenitsyn and Andrei D. Sakharov.

Few balanced minds could fail to be moved by the searing account given by Solzhenitsyn in his *The Gulag Archipelago*,[32] particularly in the second volume as published in English in 1975. It concerns one of the two great crimes committed in the twentieth century against humanity: first the Nazi extermination camps, and then the comprehensive Soviet system of destructive-labour camps for political victims. Solzhenitsyn's prefatory maps and extensive index give an indication of the scope of his work and of the soul-degrading system which he memorializes.

In the same year came the English-language edition of *From Under the Rubble*, which Solzhenitsyn edited in exile and which included contributions by six dissident colleagues who wrote within the Soviet Union at very considerable risk to themselves. "It is from out of those dank and dark depths," comments Solzhenitsyn in his Foreword to the book, "from under the rubble, that we are now putting forth our first feeble shoots. If we wait for history to present us with freedom and other precious gifts, we risk waiting in vain. History is us – and there is no alternative but to shoulder the burden of what we so passionately desire and bear it out of the depths."[33]

Meanwhile Sakharov had published a book, *Sakharov Speaks*,[34] which incorporated various of his writings on the plight of Soviet dissidents (including himself), the need for relieving the claustrophobic Soviet cultural atmosphere, and the problem of harmonizing relations with the non-Communist world. Sakharov, a brilliant physicist, had led the high-powered Soviet team which had produced the hydrogen bomb before the Americans; but from around 1958 onwards he had been increasingly concerned about what he regarded as the deteriorating situation within his own country. Following Solzhenitsyn's exile, Sakharov had become the leading spokesman for Russia's human rights still remaining within the country.

Then in 1975 Sakharov was awarded – *in absentia*, for he was not allowed to travel to receive it – the Nobel peace prize, and he was the first Russian to receive that award. In the same year came his book entitled *My Country and the World*. As he took pains to point out in the book,

> I am very fond of the landscape and culture of my country and of its people, and I am in no way eager to play the role of a 'debunker.' But I find it necessary to call attention to those negative aspects . . . that are passed over in silence by Soviet and pro-Soviet propaganda.
>
> One 'dogma of the faith' that has always figured in Soviet and pro-Soviet propaganda is the thesis of the uniqueness of the Soviet political and economic system, which (it is claimed) is the prototype for all other countries: the most just, humane, and most progressive system, ensuring the highest labor pro-ductivity, the highest standard of living, etc.
>
> The more obvious the complete failure to live up to most of the promises in that dogma, the more insistently it is maintained. . . .[35]

Meanwhile the Soviet economy continued to stagnate and the government continued to flounder. Eventually a new leader, in the shape of Mikhail Gorbachev, thrust himself into prominence. Having been born in 1931 in the Southern Soviet Union village of Privolnoe, and having by the age of 15 started work as a harvester operator, Gorbachev had by 1967 received degrees both in law and agriculture. His rise through the Communist hierarchy was swift, and by 1970 he had become a member of the USSR's Supreme Soviet, in 1983 he became General Secretary of the Communist Party of the Soviet Union, and in 1988 he was chosen as his country's President as well.

Meanwhile, in 1987, he had published his eloquent book entitled *Perestroika: New Thinking for Our Country and the*

World.[36] The book offered a fascinating combination of
astuteness together with intellectual provinciality. In the
book Gorbachev provided, at one and the same time, a
scathing denunciation of much that he found wrong in his
country plus a series of proposed remedies constructed
within the confines of an ideological straightjacket. His book
forcefully set forth what he saw as the symptoms of the Soviet
Union's malaise. In the latter part of the 1970s, he pointed
out, the country had begun to lose its momentum. Stagnation "and other phenomena alien to socialism" had
begun to appear. The economic growth rate declined. The
economic gap between the Soviet Union and what he can-
didly referred to as "the world's advanced nations" widened
still more. The consumer "found himself totally at the mercy
of the producer and had to make do with what the latter
chose to give him." Moreover, declining growth rates and
economic stagnation "were bound to affect other aspects
of the life of Soviet society." In consequence, continued
Gorbachev, "A gradual erosion of the ideological and moral
values of our people began." The situation was indeed serious. "Problems snowballed faster than they were resolved."
The country verged on crisis.[37]

Just then I was very lucky because, at the insistence of a
friend, the first of my many visits to the Soviet Union and
Russia took place, in 1985. It was then that – to his great
credit – Gorbachev was already moving in the direction of
glasnost, or openness, and *perestroika*, or restructuring.
Already the stifling claustrophobic cultural atmosphere was
beginning to change and people could breathe more freely.
Yet I recall with amusement that getting a one-page photo-
copy of a harmless document required a couple of official
signatures. Nevertheless, the atmosphere of the times was
one of growing personal liberation.

But then Gorbachev went on to display his own muddled

thinking about ideology. His particular allegiance was to Lenin, and in his *Perestroika* book he referred to Lenin *well over seventy times* – always with admiration. Yet, as we have seen, Lenin scarcely qualified to serve as a model of civilized humanity.

"*Perestroika*," Gorbachev emphasized, "is closely connected with socialism as a system." Moreover, he insisted, "I would like to point out . . . that we are conducting all our reforms in accordance with the socialist choice. We are looking within socialism, rather than outside it, for the answers to all the questions that arise. We assess our successes and errors alike by socialist standards. . . ."

"More socialism," declared Gorbachev in a slightly baffling broadside which seems to defy history, "means more democracy, openness and collectivism in production, social and personal relations among people, more dignity and self-respect for the individual." In addition, "more socialism means more patriotism and aspiration to noble ideals. . . ."[38]

"We want more socialism," said Gorbachev in a remarkable tour de force, "and, therefore, more democracy." And to avoid any possible misunderstanding he made the following sweeping assertion: ". . . We aim to strengthen socialism, not replace it with a different system. What is offered to us from the West . . . is unacceptable to us."[39]

As Service points out, there came a time when Gorbachev (as a matter of expediency or otherwise) seemed tacitly to reject Marxist-Leninist concepts. But he never did make a clean break.[40]

Gorbachev deserves enormous credit, and his place in history is assured. He presided over the dissolution of the Soviet Union and the Soviet empire. We can regard him as a transition figure between the Marxist-Leninist totalitarian tradition and a more open society. He is paradoxical in that he had some brilliant insights yet at the same time in his leadership role he showed himself as a man of limited intellectual horizons. His ideological resources became exhausted.

Boris Yeltsin, by contrast, *did* make a clean break with Marxism-Leninism. His background was rather similar to that of Gorbachev, but there came a time when Yeltsin repudiated the Communist Party. He showed himself a very brave man in the heady days that brought him, in 1991, to supreme power as President of the Russian Federation. He assembled a very bright team, and together they set about on a vigorous programme of economic reform.

The main thrust of the reform programme was to create a proper free-market economy for Russia. This included what became by far the world's largest privatization programme. In one sense this was a great success in dispersing the ownership of productive assets; but unfortunately many of those assets landed in the hands of corrupt bureaucrats or party bosses.

But the main problem with the so-called reform programme lay in its basic assumptions. It was assumed that "reform" and "free market" were more or less synonymous. Experience both in the West and in the East has shown that this is far from being necessarily the case. The cultural context is everywhere enormously important.

For a while, especially in the early and mid-1990s, things went remarkably well for Russia. Inflation steadily declined, the supermarkets were bulging with food and with customers, more and more people were able to buy privatized flats, and ever-widening car ownership provided Western-style city traffic jams and parking headaches.

But then came the East Asian meltdown; and the Asian flu hit Russia with savage severity. Unemployment and inflation soared, and soon many Russians were living below the poverty line. Russians, along with East Asians, came to realize that the vaunted Western free-market model provided no Utopia after all.

The old question reappeared: if not Communism, then what? Boris Yeltsin was among those thoughtful Russians who called for the creation of a new ideology.

From the time he became Tsar in 1696, and especially after he founded St. Petersburg in 1703, Russia's Peter the Great (1672–1725) made a determined effort to modernize Russia, and he brought in much Western expertise for this purpose. Much later, in the years leading up to World War I, Russia was industrializing very rapidly, again with the help of Western expertise. During the long period of Soviet rule, much technical advice was again provided by the West. Throughout most of the 1980s and 1990s, Gorbachev and then Yeltsin struggled – still with the aid of much expertise from the West – to modernize their ailing country with its laggard economy and underdeveloped political and social system. And that same sort of *ad hoc* advice has continued to the present day.[41]

But the West's long-continued advice to Russia has – with one major exception – been pragmatic and piecemeal. It has lacked any over-arching character. It has been devoid of any comprehensive vision.

The exception is of course Marxism. And how can we characterize Marxism as exemplified by the Great Marxist Experiment? In Conquest's summation,

> It seems clear that the sacrifices of Lenin's and Stalin's rule – running into tens of millions of deaths, and other moral and physical suffering on a vast scale – could only be justified if they had produced a society incomparably superior to anything in the Russian past, anything in the reformist West. Few would now argue that this has occurred.[42]

Notwithstanding the long-running Western pragmatic advice to Russia, the West has inflicted a terrible double injury to that vast country: on the one hand, the West deliberately exported to Russia a dangerous and defective ideological product; and on the other hand, the West has done virtually nothing to construct an adequate comprehensive ideology with particular reference to the emerging countries including Russia.

This is a grave, indeed a damning, indictment of the West. It constitutes criminal negligence.

Yet – strange as it may seem – Marxism, although fundamentally defective, may – and indeed does – contain some of the seeds of the required global ideological synthesis. It is this paradox that we shall explore in the next chapter.

V Scientific Idealism

In London a beautiful eighteenth-century building houses the Marx Memorial Library, and not surprisingly people come from all over the world to visit the library and to attend programmes in honour of the great man. Marx of course did most of his work in London and fittingly he is buried there.

Living as he did during most of the nineteenth century in Britain as the preeminent industrial nation of the day, Marx was in a perfect position to observe how the modern world was evolving. It was part of his genius that he enunciated the concept of *the productive forces* – a concept which even today many social scientists do not properly comprehend or appreciate.

Marx hinted at those forces in the following key passage in the first volume of his great work *Capital:*

> Labour is, in the first place, a process in which both man and nature participate, and in which man of his own accord starts, regulates and controls the material reactions between himself and Nature. He opposes himself to Nature as one of her own forces, setting in motion arms and legs, heads and hands, the natural forces of his body, in order to appropriate Nature's production in a form adapted to his own wants. By thus acting

on the external world and changing it, he at the same time
changes his own nature. . . . He not only effects a change of
form in the material on which he works, but he also realizes
a purpose of his own . . . to which he must subordinate his
will. . . .[1]

It shows Marx's intellectual power that he so clearly recognized the man/nature relationship and the importance of
the productive forces. He viewed the productive forces as
including (1) working people, (2) means of production as
developed and employed by people, and (3) the raw
materials and natural resources consumed in the productive
process.[2]

In the second volume of *Capital*, Marx carried his fundamental analysis further as follows:

Whatever the social form of production, labourers and means
of production always remain factors of it. But in a state of
separation from each other either of these factors can be such
only potentially. For production to go on at all they must unite.
The specific manner in which this union is accomplished distin-
guishes the different economic epochs of the structure of
society from each other.[3]

In his *The Poverty of Philosopy*, Marx likewise wrote in similar
vein:

Social relations are closely bound up with productive forces.
In acquiring new productive forces men change their mode of
production, and in changing their mode of production . . .
they change all their social relations. . . .[4]

In spite of his multi-disciplinary breadth of vision, however, Marx did go badly wrong on one crucial point.
Although he attached great importance to the productive

forces, he never fully grasped the idea that those forces would themselves be constantly and creatively reshaped by new technology. He tended to envisage a straight-line extension of the kind of machinery found in nineteenth-century factories.

At his very elbow, Marx had dramatic proof of the liveliness and versatility of nineteenth-century Western technology, for it was while he was living and labouring in London that there occurred the Crystal Palace Exhibition – or Great Exhibition, as it was properly called – of 1851.[5] It was held in London in a vast and beautiful glass structure that put to shame Britain's Millenium Dome of 2000AD.

At the Great Exhibition, arrayed in lavish profusion, were pieces of the new technology that was changing the character and fabric of Western society. One wonders if Marx left the British Museum, where he was steeped in his manuscripts, to visit the Great Exhibition. Certainly he had ample opportunity to observe the precocious technology which was transforming Western society and culture in varied and complex ways.

It was in his *A Contribution to the Critique of Political Economy* that Marx included this celebrated passage:

> The mode of production of material life conditions the social, political and intellectual life process in general. It is not the consciousness of men that determines their being, but, on the contrary, their social being determines their consciousness.[6]

It is here that we must part company with the Marxist tradition. Marxism, as the foregoing quotation dramatizes, exemplifies philosophical materialism, and Marx stood for what in that context he called Scientific Socialism. But in this book, by contrast, we have already identified our focus as Scientific Idealism.

In Chapter III we found that all truly creative artistic and literary and scientific activity is masochistic in nature; and this normally takes the form of *sublimated* masochistic activity rather than overt physical force. Isaac Newton, as we have seen, provided a perfect example of such sublimated masochistic activity.

In order to understand this more fully, we can examine another and equally durable tradition of sublimated masochistic activity – a tradition extending back even to far before Newton's time, and a tradition with the most profound social implications.

As David Kunzle indicates, as early as the mid-fourteenth century AD women and girls began to put themselves into corsets.[7] As Marianne Thesander points out in her charming book entitled *The Feminine Ideal*,[8] the early corsets included iron ones that were beautifully pierced and engraved; but boned tight-laced fabric corsets became increasingly in vogue.

Tight-laced corsets remained prevalent on through successive centuries including most of the eighteenth and nineteenth centuries. The horrors of World War I for a few years virtually killed the corset, but then it revived; and for example after World War II, in 1947, women's back-laced corsets constituted an official component of the British cost-of-living index.[9]

Young girls (for corset training started early) came to love their corsets and often chose to wear them at night as well as by day. Some clerics fulminated against the tight-laced corset on the grounds (admittedly plausible) that it stimulated amorous feminine feelings; and quite a few doctors were not amused by tight lacing, perhaps forgetting that much depended upon how exuberantly it was performed.

One woman reported that "The perfect compression of a really tight-laced corset gives me a delicious, incomparable feeling. . . ." According to another, "I have a 16-inch [about 41 cm.] waist and never have occasion to visit a physician." In the words of yet another, "My daughters have been rigorously corset-trained from childhood, and their good health speaks volumes for the practice." Beauty abounded.

As Kunzle indicates, people have often misunderstood the psychology of the tight-laced corseted woman, thinking that tight-lacing betokens female subjection. To the exact contrary, he points out, it symbolizes female power.

Female fashion is generally recognized as providing a delicate social indicator. As this is written, one need only to enter, for example, the average Western supermarket to validate that Western feminine fashion has in recent years sunk to a low ebb. In broad cultural terms, such a situation can be corrected.

The foregoing brief dicussion is relevant to our overall theme for two reasons: (1) because it illustrates the seminal and creative role of sublimated masochism in human society; and (2) because it helps to elucidate the nature and epistemology (principles of the basis of knowledge) implicit in Scientific Idealism. To this we now turn.

Philosophical idealism has a great tradition going back at least to Plato (427–347 BC). Platonic doctrine held that ideas (or forms, to use a term closer to the original Greek) – as of truth, beauty, and goodness – have a meaning of their own apart from sensory perceptions.[10] For Plato, reality consists of more than meets the eye. Society owes allegiance to higher values even if they are sometimes honoured more in the breach than in the observance. A worm's-eye "realistic" view of public problems may be miles away from reality. Man has the purposive obligation to try to realize the ideal in practice. Of course, philosophical idealism entails plenty of technicalities for the scholar's delectation, but philosophical and commonsense idealism are not unrelated.

Future historians will no doubt marvel at the dream-like way in which, without ever being conscious of the fact, many millions of Westerners could let shallow pragmatic attitudes imprison them. A key reason for that intellectual incarceration was of course the impact of nineteenth-century materialistic science.

During the nineteenth century, philosophical idealism had wilted under the onslaught of the prevailing materialistic science. Werner Heisenberg, the nuclear scientist and Nobel laureate, has thus characterized the physicist's outlook at that time:

> The world consisted of things in space and time, the things ... of matter, and matter can produce and be acted upon by forces.... Events follow from the interplay between matter and forces; every event is the result and the cause of other events....
> In this way, ... the nineteenth century developed an extremely rigid frame for natural science which formed not only science but also the general outlook of great masses of people.... Matter was the primary reality. The progress of science was pictured as a crusade of conquest into the material world.[11]

At the same time, idealism was reeling under the hammer blows of technological change. Although technology then depended much less upon pure science than it does today, the connection between the two had already been discerned, and as the century marched on, men increasingly looked to their materialistic science to provide the blessings of life. Those who preached philosophical idealism began to seem alienated from their own culture.

Yet it is true that the nineteenth-century had inherited the powerful idealism of the great George Berkeley (1685–1753). Berkeley was born of Anglo-Irish stock in or near the

town of Kilkenny, Ireland. His early years were spent at
Dysart Castle, overlooking the river Nore, where his father
was a gentleman farmer and commissioned officer.[12] Little
is known of the son's early years, but later Berkeley wrote
an account of how he and some schoolboy friends had
explored a nearby cave – thus rather reminding us of the
young Humphrey Davy's activities around a century later.

Eventually Berkeley became a somewhat controversial Fellow of Trinity College, Dublin – controversial because his
doctrines seemed to many people to defy common sense.
As it happened, Berkeley was merely far ahead of his time;
the fast-evolving natural sciences were to make his doctrines
ever more timely.

As a philosophical idealist Berkeley is perhaps best known
for his immaterialism, the belief that there is no such thing
as material substance. This is not a denial that things exist,
merely a statement that they lack substantiality. For Berkeley, everyday objects are collections of ideas or sensations.
In his own words,

> That the things I see with my eyes and touch with my hands
> do exist, really exist, I make not the least question. The only
> thing whose existence we deny is that which *philosophers* call
> Matter. . . . And in doing of this there is no damage done to
> the rest of mankind, who, I dare say, will never miss it.[13]

But Berkeley's opponents, whether of the eighteenth or
nineteenth century or today, have commonly misunderstood him as believing that everyday objects have no existence except in the mind of the human or animal beholder
or of God. Boswell recounts that the learned Dr. Johnson,
having had his fill of Berkeley's impractical nonsense, kicked
a large stone and exclaimed, "I refute him thus!" Poets

enjoyed lampooning the perspicacious philosopher's views in such verses as

> My meat and my drink
> Are but thoughts that I think.

And in deference to those who satirized him, one must admit that some of Berkeley's writings were not lacking in obscurity.

Considerably more obscure were various writings of the famous German idealists Immanuel Kant (1724–1804) and Georg Wilhelm Friedrich Hegel (1770–1831). These towering intellectuals acquired the reputation, not entirely undeserved, of ponderous thinking leading to absolutist doctrines, and Marx was by no means alone in reacting against Hegel's worship of the Prussian state.[14]

Berkeley had both scientific and mathematical qualifications, but most of the philosophers who came after him knew nothing and cared less about science, and they woefully underestimated its importance. And since the natural sciences were already remaking men's lives and thoughts, such philosophers lost touch with reality.

In 1905, as a young German-born physicist and mathematician working at the Swiss patent office in Berne, Albert Einstein (1879–1955) published a paper in which he boldly declared that energy and mass are essentially the same. The revolutionary implications of his contention can be discerned merely by placing it cheek-by-jowl with a standard dictionary definition of mass as "the quantity of matter that a body contains." By asserting the transformability of matter into energy, Einstein had undermined the whole basis of materialistic science; here was perhaps the biggest single bombshell in the entire post-Newtonian history of science – or of philosophy.[15]

In its practical implications, Einstein's paper presaged another kind of bombshell, for implicitly it carried the germinal idea of atomic (or more correctly, nuclear) weapons; if matter can in principle be transformed into energy, cannot practical means be found to break a series of atomic nuclei apart and thus release large amounts of energy?

A vast amount of work had to be done before any such wild idea could be seriously contemplated, let alone carried out; but significantly it was Einstein himself who, in his now-famous letter of October 1939 to President Franklin D. Roosevelt, outlined the possibility of a workable atomic bomb and recommended a project to create one lest the Nazis did so first. Other scientists had already addressed the US government on the subject, but it was Einstein's letter to the President that carried the day.[16] One wonders what might have been the course of history had the Nazi regime reached the scientific goal before the Allies.

As we shall see, Einstein's theory had already received laboratory confirmation through pioneering research carried out in Britain in the early 1930s. But the really shattering confirmation of Einstein's original calculation came on July 16, 1945, when the first nuclear explosion was detonated near Alamogordo, New Mexico. There for all time was proved *the utter practicality of theory* and the threadbare lack of realism of those hard-headed "realists" who spurn it. Not only would theoretical science never be the same again; the link between theory and practice, between science and its applications, had been most spectacularly demonstrated. The confirmation was then repeated by converting matter into energy for peaceful purposes, and all the world's nuclear power plants today bear witness to it.

Albert Einstein's theory – as fully confirmed both in the laboratory and in the field – harmonizes perfectly with the idealist philosophy of George Berkeley; and it is thus that we arrive at the title of the present chapter. These historic developments in philosophy, in science, and in the philosophy of science, provide an inspired interdisciplinary mix. Centuries-old arguments can be resolved, and centuries-old uncertainties can vanish.

In terms of timing, the detonation of the world's first nuclear bomb trailed some years behind portentous developments inside the edifice of physical theory. Nineteenth-century physicists had believed in two sharply divided categories of reality: material substances on the one hand, and on the other hand various kinds of fields and radiations – light, radiant heat, electricity, and magnetism, for example. The relations between the two categories, at best never clear, had become still more confused with the advent of Einstein's doctrine of the interchangeability of matter and energy. This chaotic conceptual situation gave rise, in the 1920s and 1930s, to the theory of quantum mechanics, for which the Danish scientist Niels Bohr deserves much of the credit and which most of the world's physicists have since embraced in principle.

As early as 1931, Sir James Jeans could write that "The tendency of modern physics is to resolve the whole material universe into waves, and nothing but waves."[17] Quantum theory manages to link matter (or what passes for matter) with electromagnetic fields and radiations by interpreting both kinds of phenomena as if they were waves analogous to light waves or radio waves. The theory derives its name from the observable fact, first noted by the German scientist Max Planck, that atoms emit electromagnetic energy in discrete packets or "quanta"; when investigators found that other kinds of radiation also came in packets, they were encouraged to attempt a generalized theory.

But any convincing confirmation of the theory had to await the new kind of experimental work that was also to

validate Einstein's original paper. At the renowned Cavendish Laboratory at the University of Cambridge, John (later
Sir John) (he was a great friend of mine) Cockcroft and
E. T. S. Walton built the world's first successful atom-
smashing machine, which accelerated particles to the
equivalent of nearly 400,000 volts. In 1932 they used it to
bombard a target of lithium metal with a stream of protons;
lithium atoms disintegrated and fragments of them were
actually transformed into energy as predicted by Einstein,
the results tallying exactly with his calculations of 1905.

Cockcroft and Walton received a Nobel prize for this
work, which ushered in a whole new era in fundamental
physics. Meanwhile Robert J. Van de Graaff of MIT was
following Faraday's example by constructing machines to
generate static electricity by friction; eventually he built one
to produce an energy of some 7 million volts, which he
used to accelerate particles for atom-smashing. Ernest O.
Lawrence at the University of California was employing magnetic fields to push particles around a circular race course
over and over again until, in one of his later machines, they
attained the then-unprecedented acceleration of 96 million
volts. But even this was only the beginning, for by the mid-
1960s, machines, patterned in general after Lawrence's but
with an accelerating power now augmented to billions of
volts, had been installed in a number of countries and far
bigger ones were on the drawing boards.

These high-energy machines have produced spectacular
results. In addition to providing still further verification of
Einstein's paper of 1905, they have validated quantum principles and have made possible a major new extension of
them. Whereas the so-called classical (a euphemism illustrat-
ing the pace of modern physics) quantum theory of the
1920s and 1930s dealt with the behaviour of particles orbit-
ing outside the nucleus of the atom, subsequent quantum

theory has been augmented to help explain what goes on inside the atomic nucleus itself.

The philosophical implications are enormous, and philosophers and laymen have only begun to appreciate them. The scientist, using his great accelerators in the manner of siege engines, has demolished the fortifications of nineteenth-century materialistic science and has opened the way for new interpretations of reality. He has time and again verified the principle of transmutability from the material to the immaterial. He has probed inside the atom's nucleus and has found there a new realm of fleeting, evanescent particles which hover in the hinterland between matter and energy. Thus have the scientific seeds been sown for fundamental changes in world outlook and for a reinstatement of the idealist viewpoint which provides the title for this chapter.

In earlier times philosophers would often run aground on the epistemological questions already mentioned – that is, on the relations between man as perceiver or onlooker or knower on the one hand and what was assumed to be the physical world on the other. For example, have you considered the epistemology of a horse race as seen on your television screen? Real horses have not invaded your parlour; instead, you as perceiver see forms or figures or idealizations which are correlated with live horses galloping along the race course. Or in further illustration of the epistemological problem, we can turn to these lines from a ballad about a member of the gentler sex:

> If those lips could only speak;
> If those eyes could only see;
> If those beautiful golden tresses
> Were there in reality;
> Could I only take your hand

As I did when you took my name!
But it's only a beautiful picture
In a beautiful golden frame.

Alas, she is there in form yet not in fact; but the form may possess more reality than the fleeting fact, since the poor creature seems to have passed away.

In Berkeley's day, arguments had already been raging for centuries on this obvious sort of question: Is that apple, which I think I see sitting before me, actually there? There it appears to be, sitting in its bowl as still as if it had been painted in a still life; but how do I know that it is not just a figment of my imagination? To answer such a question, one might select a body of representative citizens and ask each one to peer at the alleged apple and independently to record what he sees or thinks he sees. Such a jury must of course guard against optical illusions; but if twelve good men and true all swear that they see the apple in the flesh, we may presume it to be there.

And this method of establishing an apple's presence is not unrelated to the methods of the scientist; indeed, science habitually validates experiments by perceptual observation. To take one example, if I heat mercury in air, it becomes mercuric oxide, whose red colour I can readily observe. This experiment can be repeated in St.Petersburg, Russia or St.Petersburg, Florida or in Cambridge, England or Cambridge, Massachusetts, always with similar results confirmable by direct observation; neither the meteorological nor the political climate upsets the procedures employed.

Such direct sensory observation serves scientists in good stead, but in addition they have learned to extend their sensory awareness with the aid of instruments. Today, one need only scan the pages of scientific and technical journals to note the multiplicity of instruments characteristic of modern science; indeed, instrumentation has become a fascinating field in its own right, where pure science and technology meet with special fruitfulness. Most of these instruments were designed for the sole purpose of assisting man to make more accurate and sophisticated perceptual observations. In philosophical terms, they constitute epistemological equipment for use in scientific research and development.

In fundamental physics, two of the most interesting and useful pieces of epistemological equipment are the cloud chamber and the bubble chamber. The former was invented by the Scottish physicist C. T. R Wilson (1869–1959), who thus described how he first got the idea that led to it:

> In September 1894 I spent a few weeks in the observatory which then existed on the summit of Ben Nevis, the highest of the Scottish hills. The wonderful optical phenomena when the sun shone on the clouds surrounding the hilltop . . . greatly excited my imagination and made me wish to imitate them in the laboratory.
>
> At the beginning of 1895 I made some experiments for this purpose – making clouds by expansion of moist air. . . . Almost immediately I came across something which promised to be of more interest than the optical phenomena which I had intended to study.

At Cambridge, England, where he was then working, Wilson had found that by confining moist air in a glass cylinder with a piston and then suddenly pulling out the piston so as to expand and thus cool the air, he could generate a cloud – or perhaps one should say an English-style fog – of supersaturated air within the cylinder. He had further found that when electrons or other charged particles traversed the supersaturated air, they left tracks of water droplets which could be photographed or even seen with the naked eye.

In 1912, he published striking photographs of these cloud-chamber tracks in the proceedings of the Royal Society. Here for the first time in recorded history man had visually perceived the path of a fundamental sub-atomic particle. Wilson's beautifully simple instrument – now largely displaced for routine research – remains a treasure in the annals of scientific instrumentation; and it provides a permanent symbol of man's progress in linking himself with fundamental reality.[18]

The bubble chamber was invented in 1953 by D. A. Glaser, an Americal physicist who conceived the idea of it while watching bubbles form in a bottle of beer after he removed the cap. In principle akin to the cloud chamber, the bubble chamber employs a liquid (usually liquified hydrogen or propane) instead of moist air. The liquid is heated above its normal boiling point but placed under sufficient pressure to prevent it from boiling. As the pressure is momentarily released, and before boiling has a chance to begin, particles traversing the chamber leave tracks much like those formed in a cloud chamber.

The bubble chamber can operate much more rapidly than the cloud chamber, and very clear photographs can be obtained with it. The cloud chamber and the bubble chamber are certainly not the only means of tracking nuclear particles; for example, photographic emulsions (often prepared in the form of sandwiches or stacks of sensitized film) find use in the laboratory and can readily be sent aloft suspended from balloons to make tracks of cosmic particles. But it is especially the bubble chamber which, linked with the great accelerators, has made possible the staggering series of new-particle discoveries of recent years.

The philosophical implications are indeed far-reaching. It is through instruments like the foregoing that science has more and more achieved a happy relationship between its ideas and concepts and mathematical forms on the one hand and its sensory evidence on the other. Modern science reaps the advantages of constructive activity in the unseen world of ideas, and yet it successfully maintains contact with the commonsense world of sensations and perceptions, without which it could never validate its theories. And for the bridge between the two worlds, it relies chiefly upon instrumentation.

Indeed – both for science and for philosophy – a marvellously harmonious linkage between the ideal and the earthly-real has in recent years emerged. Modern science has indeed *demolished the theoretical basis of nineteenth-century materialist philosophy.*

Isaac Newton, as we saw earlier, was a profoundly religious man. George Berkeley, although first and foremost a philosopher, was to become Bishop of Cloyne. In the considered opinion of, for example, a physicist of the stature of Richard P. Feynman of the California Institute of Technology, a belief in the new science and in religion is now consistent.[19] In terms of religious awareness it is, as the proverb says, never too late to start.

But, especially in the West, a serious cultural cleavage has emerged. As C. P. Snow has famously observed,

In our society . . . we have lost even the pretence of a common culture. Persons educated with the greatest intensity we know can no longer communicate with each other on the plane of their major intellectual concern. This is serious for our creative, intellectual and, above all, our normal life. It is leading us to interpret the past wrongly, to misjudge the present, and to deny our hope of the future. It is making it difficult or impossible for us to take good action.[20]

Snow was writing particularly in the context of the natural sciences in relation to the humanities, and his comment applies with even more force since science has now demolished the basis for the older materialistic outlook. It is time for the citizenry to awaken.

Most people remain intellectually and emotionally *imprisoned* by the obsolete older outlook, which still permeates our culture. But this situation can be corrected. It is never too late to break out of that prison.

Science is linked not only to religion but also to art. Of this fact one could ask for no happier illustration than the doctrines of John Constable (1776–1837), who ranks as among the greatest of all landscape painters. "I hope to show," he said of his profession in one of his lectures, "that it is *scientific* as well as *poetic.*" "No doubt," he added in another lecture, "the greatest masters considered their best efforts as experiments." Later, he expanded his views as follows:

> Painting is a science, and should be considered as an inquiry into the laws of nature. Why, then, may not landscape painting be considered as a branch of natural philosophy, of which pictures are but the experiments?

The deterioration of art, said Constable, "has everywhere proceeded from similar causes, the imitation of preceding styles, with little reference to nature. In Italy, the taste was for the beautiful, but the beautiful, in the hands of the mannerists, became the insipid, and from that descended to the unmeaning." And again he referred to the "climax of absurdity to which . . . art may be carried, when led away from nature by fashion."[21]

Constable followed his own advice; for example, his clouds, which never slavishly copied nature yet were inspired by meticulous observation of actual clouds, have long been the envy of his fellow painters. In his studies of clouds, he made real contributions to natural science as well as to painting; a whole book has been written about his clouds,[22] and Britain's Royal Meteorological Society has recognized his contribution to its field.

But in addition, Constable clearly formulated – in a manner remarkably comparable with the epistemology implied by modern physics – his conception of the relation between *the ideal and the real.* Lecturing on Bourdon, a painter whose landscapes he admired, he said that they were "all poetry, visionary, romantic, abstracted"; and he quoted with approval a critic's remark that Bourdon was "the prince of dreamers, yet not without nature."

Constable's mastery of the relation between ideal and other reality emerges again in his reference to chiaroscuro, which

> may be defined as that power which creates space, we find it everywhere, and at all times in nature; opposition, union, light, shade, reflection, and refraction; all contribute to it. By this power, the moment we come into a room, we see that the chairs are not standing on the table, but a glance shows us the relative distances from the eye, though the darkest or the lightest may be the farthest off.

He believed that this power was the essence of Rembrandt's greatness and that it characterized the work of all the immortals in art.

What, he asked, "are the most sublime productions of the pencil but *selections of some of the forms of nature?*" Advising the young painter who "would leave a name behind him," Constable said that he must become nature's patient pupil and added: "The art of seeing nature is a thing almost as much to be acquired as the art of reading the Egyptian hieroglyphics."

"*We see nothing truly til we understand it,*" he declared. And in words that believers in the cause of science can fervently embrace, Constable added that "man is the intellectual inhabitant of one vast natural landscape. His nature is congenial with the elements of the planet itself, and he cannot but sympathize with its features, its various aspects, and its phenomena in all matters."[23]

It is no accident that Constable the painter and Wilson the physicist shared a preoccupation with clouds. It is no accident that Pasteur's creative chemistry and bacteriology were prefaced by painting. What we found earlier about Davy is no accident either – that in the great Coleridge's view Davy could well have exchanged his role of first chemist of his age for that of its first poet. Here one can well quote Wordsworth's penetrating prognosis: "If the time should ever come when what is now called science ... shall be ready to put on, as it were, a form of flesh and blood, the Poet will lend his divine spirit to aid the transfiguration."

As we have seen, science and philosophy, interacting together, provide the basis for a new outlook which we have designated as Scientific Idealism. To throw the new outlook into sharp relief, it is well to contrast it with a point of view that became fashionable at the waning of the twentieth century – namely, so-called post-modernism.

As Robert C. Solomon and Kathleen M. Higgins suggest, "Post-modernism isn't a philosophy. It's at best a holding pattern, perhaps a cry of despair."[24] In the words of Timothy Bewes, "Post-modernism is above all cynical. . . ."[25] The very concept of post-modernism is a fuzzy one; according to a definitive handbook of modern thought,

... Modernism was a movement of many segments, directions, and inner disputes; so is post-modernism, though it is harder, being contemporary, to identify. It is a still amorphous body of developments and directions marked by eclecticism, pluriculturism, and often a post-industrial, hi-tech frame of reference coupled with a sceptical view of technical progress. ... To date it remains best seen as a complex map of late 20th-century directions rather than a clearcut aesthetic and philosophical ideology.[26]

One of the most prolific and influential of the post-modernist authors is Fredric Jameson, who writes in a pleasant and easy style. His *The Cultural Turn*,[27] as published in 1998, provides an excellent example of his work. The book contains a combination of warmed-over Marxism together with a plethora of ad hoc observations on this and that; regrettably it contains no original ideological content whatever. One is driven to agree with the characterizations of post-modernism mentioned above.

More fruitful approaches can be found. Some years ago, for example, I arranged for the endowment of a lectureship in America in memory of Robert Noyce, a brilliant former student of mine who was both the father of the microprocessor and one of the founders of Silicon Valley. But this lectureship has a difference: it is not to be devoted to science as such but rather to the *strategy and tactics* of scientific research, including ethical aspects.

We shall soon see more of how such strategies and tactics can best be deployed in aid of mankind. Our goal should be to combine the vision of an Isaac Newton with that of a George Berkeley and that of a John Constable. Their wisdom, and that of their counterparts and successors, can be consolidated under the ideology which we have identified as Scientific Idealism. We have also identified the secret creative spark which actuates their efforts.

Thus – as we shall see more fully in the next chapter – we arrive at a working ideology for the dawning century and beyond. It can become a living, growing movement.

VI The Global Synthesis

As suggested in the Preface to this book, the much-publicized so-called Third Way is actually a dated and obsolete concept. It represents the reappearance of the simplistic end-of-ideology thinking which we have already examined in Chapter II.

It is useful to scrutinize the latter-day manifestations of that concept. For example, as we have seen, 1998 saw the publication of a book by Anthony Giddens, who was widely regarded as a guru of Britain's Prime Minister Tony Blair. The book, entitled *The Third Way: The Renewal of Social Democracy*,[1] immediately became fashionable in certain circles on both sides of the Atlantic; and President Bill Clinton and his wife Hillary promptly jumped on the bandwagon.

Giddens has a pleasant writing style and he comes across as an agreeable and civilized man – as of course Bill Clinton and Tony Blair do too. But in the words of the prestigious London-based journal *The Economist*, as already noted above in the Preface,

> . . . This book is awsomely, magisterially and in some ways disturbingly vacuus.
> Why disturbingly? There are many bad books in the world. But the third way is not just a parlour game for intellectuals

puzzling over the content of politics now that both socialism and 'unbridled capitalism' are in disrepute. It has become the quasi-official political philosophy of Britain's governing party. . . .[2]

An inspection of the Giddens book brings few surprises. With minor adjustments it could just as well have been written in the 1960s. Obviously it is true that the work was written after, rather than before, the collapse of the Soviet Union, but various third way or middle way approaches were topics of conversation before that collapse and even in the 1960s.

A noteworthy feature of the Giddens book is that its useful index contains *not one reference* to ideology or philosophy. The same applies to Tony Blair's book entitled *New Britain*.[3] The Blair book does touch on religion, but its approach is mainly anecdotal.

Near the end of his book, Giddens makes a brave confession. Referring to Blair's landslide victory at the polls, Giddens comments that "many who praise the scale of the victory also see the New Labour project as an empty one. . . . New Labour is widely seen as depending on media-orientated politics, and as creating 'designer socialism.' Personal images, symbolic stagings, sound bites, visual gags all count for more than issues, arguments, projects and the evaluation of campaign promises."[4] But Giddens hoped that "a substantive agenda" was emerging from the social democratic debates.[5]

That remained to be seen. In the words of one commentary, the Big Idea in the Third Way doctrine is that *there is no Big Idea.*[6] That describes the situation exactly.

The situation finds further illustration in Blair's tract entitled *The Third Way*, as published in 1998. Blair leads off by proclaiming that "I have always believed that politics is first and foremost about ideas."[7] But nothing in the way of a Big Idea emerges. One is led to believe that he cannot understand or appreciate the difference between *ad hoc* ideas on the one hand and coherent thought-systems on the other. He is imprisoned by intellectual parochialism. Our great scientists would never have been guilty of such a crime.

But let it be noted that Blair as an individual cannot be held fully responsible for this; he merely reflects the mind-contracting pragmatic fixation which was so prevalent at the end of the departing twentieth century. The dawning century will bring with it a marked intellectual improvement.

Fortunately the world is even now not devoid of Big Ideas which can benefit mankind. Taken together, certain of these Big Ideas constitute representative components of the Fourth Way which provides the title for this book. They form key ingredients of an intellectual system. They include (1) the social application of science; (2) human rights benchmarks; (3) the role of English; (4) the Keynesian legacy; (5) the international mixed economy; and (6) the cultural revolt.

The Social Application of Science. James Bryant Conant, who was both President of Havard University and a Nobel laureate in chemistry, ranked as a master of the strategy and tactics of science. Among other things he employed a splendid concept in the shape of *the constants of nature.* At a certain temperature, water freezes into ice. At another temperature, water turns into steam. Some metals are hard, others soft. Metals combined into alloys acquire different properties. Some materials conduct electricity better than others. Seeds can be made to germinate. Plants require a certain minimum temperature in order to grow.

Conant played a prominent role in the Manhattan Project which created the world's first nuclear bomb. As he later wrote,

In the early days of the work on atomic energy there was a possibility that *the constants of nature* would be such that atomic energy for power would be possible, but an atomic explosion impossible. We all hoped that this would be the case.[8]

Of course all such hopes came to nothing. The threat of the Nazi war machine required the creation of a crash programme of research and development which in the event was fraught with success. I knew a scientist – and his case was by no means unique – who, after helping to perfect the bomb, in remorse abandoned nuclear physics and turned to music, which he taught in the hope of atoning in some slight measure for the spectacular accomplishments of his original profession.

Conant likewise enunciated a paradoxical principle with the most far-reaching implications for science and its social application. "We can put it down as one of the principles learned from the history of science," he wrote, "that *a theory is only overthrown by a better theory*, never by contradictory facts."[9] Obsolete theories, whether in the natural or the social sciences, *cannot be dislodged merely by conflicting evidence*. Only a new and demonstrably superior theory will upset the antiquated one.

This Conant principle finds beautiful illustration in the work of Pasteur. Countless prestigious people attacked Pasteur until his germ theory proved itself superior. The brilliantly-unconventional work of John Maynard Keynes likewise offers, as we shall see, another splendid example.

The constants of nature can of course interact with man in a variety of ways. My father knew the Wright Brothers and he had long discussions with them about their studies of the flight of birds. In 1903 my father was present near Kitty Hawk, North Carolina, when the brothers made the first successful powered flight. In that case the constants of nature decreed – in flat contradiction to the opinions of many experts – that heavier-than-air vehicles could fly. The consequences have of course been incalculable.

During the twentieth century science became ever more prolific in its output, with implications for both good and ill. We have already mentioned man's amazing ability to create fresh problems faster than he can solve existing ones – mainly because of science and technology. As early as 1927, Britain's Bishop of Ripon, speaking to an audience of scientists, seriously proposed a moratorium on scientific research throughout the world to allow time for social adjustment to the impact of science.[10]

Far from heeding the Bishop's plea, the West and the world have relentlessly pressed on with tempting research and development projects in fields including weapons of mass destruction and the genetic manipulation of plants and animals not overlooking the possibility of cloning man himself.

As the Duke of Edinburgh has cogently expressed it,

the sort of power which mankind has gained through science demands an equally great sense of responsibility. . . . Instead of letting science have an indiscriminate and haphazard impact upon the world we must learn to use its power to create the sort of environment in which mankind can thrive and prosper.

We are, he points out, "beginning to realize that unless we are very careful indeed we can make serious and long-lasting mistakes *in the indiscriminate application of scientific techniques.*"[11] And what is the opposite of the indiscriminate application of scientific techniques? It is their discriminating application. And how can such techniques be applied with discrimination? This can be done only with due regard to the constants or laws of nature and to the moral and social needs of mankind.

The University of Cambridge is of course well over 700 years old; and Lord Ashby, who was both a leading scientist and Master of Cambridge's Clare College, pointed out that for six-sevenths of her entire history the University was focused squarely on philosophical and religious values and that only in the last seventh had this not been the case. The inference was that it might again become the case, and that this would contribute to social responsibility in science.

Before proceeding further, a reminder is in order. The six representative Big Ideas must not be treated as a mere enumeration. To the contrary, they should be viewed as some of the key components of an integrated *system*. This will become more apparent as we proceed.

Human Rights Benchmarks. The battle for human rights has been a long and honourable one. For example, these were among the commitments made by King John in Britain as early as 1215 AD:

> No man shall be taken or imprisoned or disseized [i.e. deprived of his lands] or in any way destroyed, nor will we go upon him nor put upon him, except by the lawful judgement of his peers or the law of the land.[12]

Considerably later, when Thomas Jefferson drafted the Declaration of Independence in 1776, he created another major milestone along the road to human rights. "We hold these truths to be self-evident," said the now-familiar words, "that all men are created equal, that they are endowed by their Creator with certain Rights, that among these are Life, Liberty and the pursuit of Happiness. . . ." In order to secure such rights, "Governments are instituted among Men, deriving their just powers from the consent of the governed. . . ."[13]

In the Bill of Rights, as ratified in 1791 as an addendum to the Constitution of the United States of America, one finds a number of safeguards against Federal encroachment upon essential human rights. The Congress, for example, "shall make no law respecting an establishment of religion, or prohibiting the free exercise thereof, or abridging the freedom of speech, or of the press, or the right of the people peacefully to assemble, and to petition the government for a redress of grievances." And again, "The right of the people to be secure in their persons, houses, papers, and effects, aganst unreasonable searches and seizures, shall not be violated. . . ." Likewise, "Excessive bail shall not be required, nor excessive fines imposed, nor cruel and unusual punishments inflicted."[14]

On the whole, and with occasional lapses, these safeguards have been maintained intact in America for more than two centuries. They have of course been supplemented by numerous statutes which have in turn reflected changing conditions and fresh hazards. It is especially relevant to note the growing American awareness of the relationship between economic and political rights. President Theodore Roosevelt (1858–1919) won fame for wielding the big stick against private corporate power, yet he called upon government "both to secure justice from, and to do justice to, the great corporations. . . ."[15]

President Franklin D. Roosevelt (1882–1945) reiterated the duty of government to engage in economic intervention in spite of the American *laissez faire* tradition. More than any previous American president he emphasized the intimacy of the relationship between economic and political rights; for example, one finds this theme well underlined in his famous Four Freedoms declaration of 1941 as part of his State of the Union address to Congress:

In the future days, which we seek to make secure, we look forward to a world founded upon four essential human freedoms.

The first is freedom of speech and expression – everywhere in the world.

The second is freedom of every person to worship God in his own way – everywhere in the world.

The third is freedom from want – which, translated into world terms, means economic understandings which will secure to every nation a healthy peacetime life for its inhabitants – everywhere in the world.

The fourth is freedom from fear – which, translated into world terms, means . . . that no nation will be in a position to commit any act of physical aggression against any neighbor – anywhere in the world.[16]

A most remarkable document was the Universal Declaration of Human Rights, as approved in 1948 by the United Nations General Assembly without a single dissenting vote (but with certain countries for obvious reasons choosing to abstain). Drafted to provide "a common standard of achievement for all peoples and all nations," the Universal Declaration contains thirty fundamental articles of which the following excerpts are indicative:

All human beings are born free and equal in dignity and rights. . . . Everyone has the right to life, liberty and security of person. All are equal before the law and are entitled without any discrimination to equal protection of the law. . . . No one shall be subjected to arbitrary interference with his privacy, home or correspondence, nor to attacks upon his honour or reputation. Everyone has the right to the protection of the law against such interference or attacks.

Obviously in some countries such human rights as the foregoing are honoured more in the breach than in the observance, and this likewise holds true of the following additional rights as contained in the Universal Declaration:

> Everyone has the right to own property alone as well as in association with others. . . . No one shall be arbitrarily deprived of his property. . . . Everyone has the right to freedom of thought, conscience and religion. . . . Everyone has the right to freedom of opinion and expression; this right includes freedom to hold opinions without interference and to seek, receive and impart information and ideas through any media and regardless of frontiers. . . . Everyone has the right to take part in the government of his country, directly or through freely chosen representatives. . . . The will of the people shall be the basis of the authority of government; this will shall be expressed in periodic and genuine elections which shall be by universal and equal suffrage and shall be held by secret vote or by equivalent free voting procedures.[17]

The battle for human rights is an ongoing and never-ending one. Here we are dealing with a really Big Idea. To illustrate the complex nature of the problem, the following case study may prove useful.

Following the Japanese World War II invasion of Burma – when the invaders flouted human rights in every possible way – and following the bitter and successful British and Allied campaign to expel the Japanese from Burma, the country was in desperate need of reconstruction.

A major New York City consulting engineering company asked me to go out to Burma as one of an interdisciplinary team to prepare, with US financial assistance, a national development plan for Burma. In retrospect the plan was a thoroughly sound one, and Burma's then Prime Minister U Nu gave orders for its implementation. The catch came when the Minister of Defence staged a coup and took over the government. He was such a doctrinnaire Marxist that he nationalized everything even including pushcart peddlers, and in spite of the efforts of brave dissidents the country has not recovered even to the present day. Burma (or Myanmar) has remained a desperately deprived country.

At a meeting of the American Political Science Association in San Francisco, I presented a paper entitled "The Primacy of the Political." The paper delineated ways in which human rights dramas are played out in the prevailing political context whether in Burma or otherwise.

In Chapter IV we considered the work of Solzhenitsyn and Sakharov as brave individual champions of human rights. Many organizations are likewise now involved. In addition to the United Nations in its human rights role, there are of course numerous official and voluntary human rights organizations worldwide; and Amnesty International represents a powerful global force in the human rights field. The broadcasters such as the BBC and CNN, with their enormous global audiences, have the ability to shame regimes into improving their performance. Likewise the Internet is obviously highly significant.

It is indicative, for example, that when NATO forces bombed Yugoslavia in 1999, the main and proper justification given involved violations of human rights by the government of Yugoslavia. The battle for human rights continues apace.

The Role of English. The English language has come to play a key role in the way the world conducts its affairs and activities. It is useful to consider how this situation has evolved. As Robert Burchfield points out, "no languageless society has ever been discovered" on this Earth.[18] Ideally the unity of the nations would seem to imply a linguistic unity, and this brings to mind a Biblical passage in the shape of Genesis 10–11. It appears that, after the Flood, the descendents of Noah spread abroad and founded diverse nations. At that time all the nations had a single unified language. Then various of the nations decided to build a fine new city including a huge tower – probably a so-called ziggurat – with its top in the heavens. The Lord, having come down to see the city, and having evidently decided that the people were getting above themselves, decided to take action accordingly. The Lord said,

> Behold, they are one people, and they have all one language; and this is only the beginning of what they will do; and nothing that they propose to do now will be impossible for them. Come, let us go down, and there confuse their language that they may not understand one another's speech. So the Lord scattered them abroad from there all over the face of the Earth, and they left off building the city. Therefore its name was called Babel, because there the Lord confused the language of all the Earth. . . .[19]

The Lord's penalty has been a long-lasting one, for the confusion of languages has complicated global communications ever since. For example, the BBC World Service, the Voice of America, and Radio Moscow understandably feel obliged to broadcast in a wide diversity of languages. Many of these languages – French and Spanish to take but two of numerous examples – are beautiful ones; but the quest naturally continues for a greater degree of linguistic unity.

Although the same two illustrative languages are spoken very widely over the face of the Earth, it is English which increasingly serves as the linguistic common denominator. Anybody who has travelled widely can testify that wherever he goes he is likely to find people who speak English, and as the years go by this becomes ever more apparent. In the same way, and in percentage terms, more and more scientific papers, books, computer programmes, and musical lyrics are published in English. It is English which has become the preeminent international language.

As Simeon Potter points out, "The variety of its . . . vocabulary makes English more, and not less, adaptable as a medium of world communication. English now has the richest vocabulary in the world, over two hundred thousand words, apart from compounds and derivatives, being in common use."[20]. According to Robert McCrum, William Cran and Robert MacNeil in their definitive *The Story of English*, ". . . English at the end of the twentieth century is more widely scattered, more widely spoken and written, than any other language has ever been. It has become the language of the planet, the first truly global language." English they add, "has a few rivals, but no equals." For example,

> . . . Three-quarters of the world's mail, and its telexes and cables[and no doubt its faxes and Internet messages as well] are in English. So are half of the world's technical and scientific periodicals; it is the language of technology from Silicon Valley to Shanghai. English is the medium for 80 percent of the information stored in the world's computers. Nearly half of all business deals in Europe are conducted in English. It is the language of sports and glamour: the official language of the Olympics and the Miss World competition. English is the official voice of the air, the sea, and of Christianity: it is the official ecumenical language of the World Council of Churches. Five of the largest broadcasting companies in the world . . . transmit in English. . . .[21]

English has now become "a global language with a supranational momentum." Apart from the many millions of people who are native English-speakers, "English is now everyone's second language, and has a life of its own in totally non-English situations." Many is the time that I have stayed in hotels in the Middle East or the Far East or Africa and have noted that guests from the Continent of Europe or from Latin America, for example, have perforce spoken only in English to the hotel staff or to government officials or businessmen or academics. English is indeed the pre-eminent cross-cultural language.

Scientists the world over find it easier to get along with each other when they know English.[22] According to Robert Burchfield, as Chief Editor of the celebrated multi-volume *Oxford English Dictionary*, "any literate educated person on the face of the globe is deprived if he does not know English."[23] Not surprisingly, "In virtually every country in the world foreigners are learning English to enable them to speak across frontiers in a language most likely to be understood by others."[24]

English, then, is a world language of unique richness and vitality. But it is also a language of enormous power in a very special sense. Although it would be totally absurd to contend that English is the only language capable of expressing democratic concepts, it is nonetheless superlatively equipped for this role. English can indeed be called the language of democracy, and it was Winston Churchill who especially championed this identification. "We must," he said, "never cease to proclaim in fearless tones the great principles of freedom and the rights of man, which are the joint inheritance of the English-speaking world. . . ."[25]

The London-based English-Speaking Union, in which Churchill played a prominent role, today has branches or representatives in more than forty countries. The University of Cambridge sends its English examinations to more than 150 countries. The English language, and its associated international cultural linkages, can provide a powerful component of Scientific Idealism.

The Keynesian Legacy. John Maynard Keynes, (1883–1946)

can be called the Isaac Newton of the social sciences. Keynes was indeed fascinated by Newton, whom he referred to as "This strange spirit, who was tempted by the Devil to believe he could reach all the secrets of God and Nature by the pure power of mind. . . ." Keynes purchased a large collection of Newton's papers, which was to shed much light on Newton's life and work.[26]

Keynes grew up in Cambridge, England, where his father, Neville Keynes, was a professor of economics and for fifteen years served as the University of Cambridge's chief administrative officer. The son went to Eton, received his Cambridge degree, served for a time in the India office, wrote a book on probability theory, and became a fellow of King's College, Cambridge.

During the First World War Keynes showed his financial capability at the British Treasury, and in 1919 he was selected as a member of the British Delegation to the Paris Peace Conference. Out of this came his book *The Economic Consequences of the Peace*,[27] which earned him an enduring reputation. The book argued that the ruinous reparations imposed upon Germany – against Keynes's own strong objections at the peace conference – spelled dire trouble ahead. It seems more than likely that if Keynes's recommendations had been followed, Hitler would never have risen to power and a Second World War would not have erupted just over twenty years later. Such were the enormous stakes.

In 1925 Keynes married Lydia Lopokova, a charming Russian ballerina from St. Petersburg (my favourite of all cities), and they remained deeply in love until his death in 1946. Together they planned what was to become the celebrated Cambridge Arts Theatre, which opened in 1936. Meanwhile Keynes was already working on the book which was to usher in the Keynesian Revolution. As one source expressed it about Keynes, "It is entirely typical of him that he should have started building his theatre while he was still writing the book which would revolutionize economics" – namely *The General Theory of Employment, Interest and Money.* As he had remarked to Lydia in 1924, "The mind quickly becomes stale and infertile (at least mine does) if it thinks only about one matter."[28]

As John Kenneth Galbraith (one of my old teachers) pointed out in 1975, *The General Theory,* as first published in 1936,[29] was "the most influential book on economic and social policy so far this century,"[30] and that assessment indeed now applies to the end of the century and beyond. It is true, as Galbraith elsewhere observes, that Hitler, after he seized power, had used deficit financing to help Germany's recovery and it is true that some Swedish economists had already given serious thought to the subject; but it was Keynes who, in *The General Theory,* first developed a full-blown intellectual system.

Keynes, as Robert Skidelsky has noted, had "a luminous and mysterious mind," and his *The General Theory* is "a work of enduring fascination."[31] As with all revolutionary theories, acceptance of *The General Theory* did not come over-night – far from it. We have already considered the wonderful work done by Herbert Hoover in saving literally millions of people from death by starvation. At that time Hoover was US Secretary of Commerce. He then went on to take office as President of the United States (1929–1933); and that virtually coincided with Black Monday of 1929 and America's plunging into the depths of depression. Hoover's reaction was predictable in the light of the accepted wisdom of the time. The President, along with business leaders and other men of influence, broadcast to the people to assure them that the economy was – to use a favourite expression – "fundamentally sound," and that confidence should be maintained. Hoover patiently explained to the people that a country is like a family; when revenues fall, naturally expenditures must be reduced.

Because of its sharply reduced revenues, the Federal government naturally felt obliged to slash payrolls, and a good case in point was the great US National Bureau of Standards, which over the years had done much important scientific research and development. In accordance with accepted doctrine, leading scientists and engineers there were summarily fired. A scientist would then go home and tell his wife what had happened and they would wonder what to do next. He would then sign on for one of the so-called "make-work" unemployment relief projects.

A good friend and deputy director of the National Bureau of Standards later told me this parable. Some of the unemployed scientists were recruited as stonemasons to help build a retaining wall in the large grounds of the NBS. My friend the deputy director inspected the work and noted that it was not very good. He and his colleagues wondered how the scientists might be made more productive, and it was then that they had an intellectual breakthrough: the scientists should be reassigned to their original jobs! And so in due course they were.

But that sort of lesson took much time to sink in. Even after Franklin D. Roosevelt assumed office as President in 1933, the same pre-Keynesian mentality continued to prevail. In the December 31, 1933 issue of *The New York Times*, Keynes published an Open Letter to the President in which he urged "overwhelming emphasis on the increase of national purchasing power resulting from government expenditure, which is financed by loans." In the following year Keynes had what Galbraith describes as a rather unsatisfactory personal meeting with the President.[32] It was not until the 1936 publication of *The General Theory* that things really began to come alight; and the policy consequences were profound. As Skidelsky puts it, "The intellectual conversion of all the younger British and American economists started soon after *The General Theory* was published; Keynesian fiscal policy began to be used in 1940 in the United States and in 1941 in Britain." And he refers to "Keynes who above all sought to influence policy. . . ."[33]

As Paul A. Samuelson and William D. Nordhaus point out in their definitive book *Economics* – a work which sets a real world standard for economics – "the science of *macroenomics* is concerned with the overall performance of the economy." Macroeconomics, they add,

did not even exist in its modern form until . . . John Maynard Keynes published his revolutionary *General Theory of Employment, Interest and Money*. At the time England and the United States were still stuck in the Great Depression of the 1930s, and over one-quarter of the American labor force was unemployed. In his new theory Keynes developed an analysis of what causes unemployment and economic downturns, how investment and consumption are determined, how central banks manage money and interest rates, and why some nations thrive while others stagnate. Keynes also argued that governments have an important role in smoothing out the ups and downs of business cycles. Although macroeconomics has progressed far since his first insights, the issues addressed by Keynes still define the study of macroeconomics today.[34]

It is significant, as D. E. Moggridge points out, that Keynes's economist predecessors at Cambridge – including his economist father Neville Keynes – all regarded economics as a *moral* science.[35] Part of John Maynard Keynes's own genius of course lay in his multidisciplinary approach to everything. There lay the route to his brilliant insights. Not only the insights themselves, but also his inspired means for reaching them, indicate that he and his methods should form part of any intellectual synthesis.

The International Mixed Economy. Earlier I worked at two of Nigeria's leading universities – the University of Ibadan and the University of Ife – in the field of public administration. The universities are situated on beautiful campuses which by a happy coincidence were designed in London.

Nigeria has for many years enjoyed the reputation of being one of the most corrupt countries in Africa or indeed in the world. Yet the Nigerian people are delightful and have a wonderful sense of humour. When civilian government was re-established in Nigeria in 1999, people naturally hoped that corruption might disappear; but over many years, and regardless of regime, corruption has remained endemic in Nigeria. Both Christianity and Islam are very strong in Nigeria and that has no doubt strengthened family values, but it has by no means eliminated corruption. The level of corruption has for many years retarded the country's economic development.

The level of corruption in Japan played a major role in the meltdown there in 1998. From there the Asian contagion spread rapidly and among other places hit with devastating effect in Indonesia with her some 200 million people. I have given a great deal of consulting advice in that beautiful country, about which I wrote a book.[36] Indonesia enjoyed more than twenty years of non-stop economic growth until the Asian disease brought a ruinous impact, with the currency quickly losing more than 80 percent of its value. The Indonesian collapse also brought revelations of huge corruption.

The Asian contagion then spread on into Russia, where again it brought a financial collapse accompanied by much suffering among ordinary people. In all of the foregoing instances, a rudderless psychology prevailed among both policy-makers and the citizenry. In Russia there has been a dramatic resurgence in the church, but that has by no means solved the problem of a guiding philosophy, although it may contribute towards an eventual solution.

The West has extended vast amounts of financial and technical assistance to such countries as Nigeria and Indonesia and Russia. Much of this aid has taken the form of large-scale loans from the International Monetary Fund (IMF) and the International Bank for Reconstruction and Development (IBRD) for projects which have often been ill-advized and accompanied by corruption in both the placing of contracts and their implementation. Many observers think that the IMF needs a thorough reorganization; and George Soros has suggested that it should be converted into a proper international bank designed to safeguard the global monetary system.[37]

Because so many of the developing countries already have large outstanding international loans, and because the ordinary populace are often suffering much privation, well-meaning people have frequently suggested that such loans should simply be cancelled. For example, in 1999, the Secretary-General of the British Commonwealth of Nations called for "a complete write-off of external debt" for a number of the developing countries on the grounds that debt service was causing much hardship among ordinary people.[38] But such write-offs typically serve mainly to reward corruption. With the common people in mind, it is kinder and more constructive never to forgive international loans without strict conditions *for prior reform*. Unconditional cancellation of external debts brings smiles to the corrupt!

A Russian economist friend of mine, noting the enormous leakages from Western loans to Russia, says that all Western-funded projects in Russia should be directly controlled and managed by resident Western experts. Experience supports him.

From its headquarters in New York City, the United Nations operates an international network of specialized agencies which provide technical assistance in a wide variety of fields. These include, for example, the World Health Organization, the Food and Agriculture Organization, and the United Nations Industrial Development Organization. I have known a number of the staff of such organizations, and they are often able and experienced and committed people – within the confines of their special fields.

America, Britain, France, Germany and other Western countries likewise have valuable bilateral aid programmes for helping the less-developed countries. I have known many such Western aid officials, and I have a high regard for what is often their real dedication. But their whole approach is essentially pragmatic and piecemeal and fails to transform the situation. I am pleased and proud to be a Life Member of the Washington-based Society for International Development, which sponsors many studies on developmental matters; but the same characterization applies.

America's Peace Corps and Britain's Voluntary Service Overseas have also done much valuable educational and other work in third-world countries. Pioneering organizations in the field likewise include British Executive Service Overseas and the US-based International Executive Service Corps, both of which, with the help of business and government funding, send experts in many specific fields to give advice in newly-developing countries.

A particularly interesting kind of aid programme is that of the British-based Intermediate Technology Development Group, which tries to get away from the giantism of many costly, and often ineffective, Western aid projects in favour of adapting the latest technology to small-scale applications. The ITDG has projects in many developing countries and it has shown a strong track record.

Yet all of this having been said, something is still obviously missing.

When Nikita Khruschev, referring to the capitalist world, declared "We will bury you!", he had a vision, and millions of people worldwide shared that vision. The vision, true enough, was a defective one, but it was real and dynamic and compelling.

For example, I have a Russian friend, an engineer, who in Soviet days was sent with his family to Yemen as part of the Soviet Union's worldwide programme of technical and ideological assistance. As it happened my friend was not a Communist, but he was caught up in the spirit of the Soviet global initiative. He was in Yemen not just to provide clean water and rural electrification; he and his team were also equipped to offer intellectual assistance.

Marxism may not have provided a proper intellectual answer, but in its day it commanded a huge following reaching to every continent. Another and more durable form of intellectual assistance is now required. An ideological vacuum will not suffice.

The Cultural Revolt. One reason why so many people do not understand what is missing in their lives is because of the "dumbing down"[39] so prevalent in contemporary Western popular culture. Russia, by contrast, has such an immensely rich popular culture. It is already under assault by Western soap operas and other intrusions, yet a large measure of cultural integrity remains – but for how long?

One is more and more struck by the mediocrity and triviality of Western popular culture including most of the output of the media. One is equally struck by the vacuousness of most academic cultural research or pseudo-research in this period of post-modern limbo.

The youth of many countries have been affected accordingly. As Roger Scruton expresses it,

Among youth, as we know it from our modern cities, a new human type is emerging. It has its own language, its own customs, its own territory and its own self-contained economy. It also has its own culture – a culture which is largely indifferent to traditional boundaries, traditional loyalties, and traditional forms of learning.

Moreover, those who belong to the new human type find themselves trapped "in a culture of near inarticulateness."[40] Such is the plight of much of post-modern youth, especially in the West. Here we see the growing risk of international cultural contamination – the spread of a deadly virus. To change the figure of speech, here we see the effluent of an ever-more-homogenized popular culture – one that is uncreative, and boring.

Fortunately there are countervailing forces – not least in the perception that something is wrong. For example, one can consider the imperial city of St. Petersburg, Russia – imperial not only in terms of its history but also by virtue of its beauty and its cultural stature. The city possesses what, in the shape of the Hermitage,[41] is arguably the world's finest art museum. The city has, in the Kirov, what is undoubtedly the world's leading ballet company. The city has vast interdisciplinary wealth in research institutions in the natural sciences and engineering. And the city is well described in a cherished and plausible proverb which says this: the best ideas come from St. Petersburg.

The proverb embraces many things. For example, the skirt for women is certainly one of the greatest inventions in recorded history. St. Petersburg women – not all of them but many of them – wear their skirts beautifully, and they know how to flaunt them in a most seductive way. Many of the women also show their artistry by doing their own dressmaking – all the more valuable in times of economic uncertainty. I know a St. Petersburg fashion designer who has her own large salon and whose clients include a New York City fashion chain which exports her dresses to diverse countries – including Russia! St. Petersburg needs Western capital and management expertise to play her proper role in this tempting field.

But St. Petersburg's most important role is that of a great cultural and economic bridge between East and West. She has indeed always played this role, from her founding in 1703 onwards. During the terrible siege of 1941–1944, the Nazis made every effort to extinguish that noble city but without success.

St. Petersburg, with her some five million people, is the largest city between London and Moscow. She is far and away Russia's biggest general cargo port; and in addition she is a major centre for transport by air, inland waterway, and rail, as well as being a key focal point for international telecommunications. But most important of all, she is an East-West cultural gateway in just the manner that Peter the Great originally intended.

So if alien cultural barbarians are at the gates, St. Petersburg is in a strategic position to deal with them. But actually, as history has repeatedly shown, it often makes more sense to convert the barbarians rather than to rely only on overt means. Thus, when Alexander the Great invaded Iran, he showed wisdom when he encouraged his officers to acquire Persian wives, who he thought would have a civilizing influence.

I have not the slightest doubt that the Russians, with their surpassingly rich culture and their unquenchable sense of humour, can aid all of us in our quest. The post-modernist cultural barbarians can be helped to embrace a creative synthesis.

If you have a friend who is only partially sighted, you want to help him in every way you can. But unless his sight can be corrected, his perception of reality is bound to be different from yours. On the other hand, your friend may have such a vivid imagination that he may have a fuller awareness of true reality than you do. Perhaps you and he can complement each other.

As we have seen, the real scientist, in whatever field, operates in both the observed and the unseen worlds. That was certainly true with, for example, Isaac Newton and John Maynard Keynes. Unless we can operate in both realms, we are incomplete people.

Earlier in this chapter we considered the limitations of people who have no Big Ideas. Without such Big Ideas, we are gravely handicapped. But why? Why do we need Big Ideas? Why not try to dispense with them?

Very briefly – for anybody who doesn't already see the point – a philosophy of science can help to guide both scientific research and the discriminating application of science for man's welfare. A theoretical rationale of human rights can help to apply them in practice. The English language can be studied and cherished both as a repository of wisdom and as a practical means of day-to-day communication. The Keynesian legacy can be considered both as a major key to the social sciences and as a source of guidance on, for example, interest rates and money flows. The international mixed economy can be examined both as a global economic system and as a source of clues on, for example, fighting corruption. The revolt against popular culture can be viewed as a crucial matter of preserving our cultural heritage or as an entertaining and pathetic social phenomenon. Theory and practice interact. And as Einstein proved for all time, there is nothing more practical than theory.

No Big Ideas means a dull and monochromatic world. But Big Ideas can bring excitement and verve to life. The role of the true intellectual becomes clear. He can help to uncover such ideas and, in the spirit of Pasteur, he can offer guidance in their application in aid of mankind.

In the preceding chapter we suggested Scientific Idealism as the new intellectual's most productive working philosophy for the twenty-first century. Meanwhile – again in the spirit of Pasteur in his dealings with his many opponents – the new intellectual can lead in vanquishing or converting the cultural barbarians in our midst – both for their sake and for ours.

This, then, is the Fourth Way, which can spread its wings. We have been on an intellectual journey together, and further adventures lie ahead.

Russia now finds herself in vigorous ideological ferment, and this often takes a creative interdisciplinary form. At the same time – and in spite of its deadening over-specialization tendencies in recent years – the West is not devoid of interdisciplinary ideological resources. An intellectual interaction between East and West can greatly facilitate ideological progress.

Here the global Internet – if it is used with great care and discrimination – can play a pivotal role. The website which accompanies this book can be brought to bear, and so can other websites with which it can be linked. Readable and coherent printed materials can be generated to augment the supply of interdisciplinary knowledge.

As the world's problems continue to multiply, the cause of global intellectual reconstruction becomes ever more pressing. With courage and with a spirit of adventure, we can prove that this reconstruction is an attainable goal! Here, indeed, we face the challenge of the age!

*   *   *

Notes

CHAPTER I VISION AND BLINDNESS

1 *The Times* (London), 30 September 1997, p. 13.
2 Quoted by George Scott-Moncrieff, in "Edinburgh and Her Golden Age," *Scottish Field*, Vol. CXX, No.848 (August 1973), p. 16.
3 *The Times* (London), *Interface*, 24 September 1997, p. 16.
4 Idem.
5 David Shenk, *Data Smog: Surviving the Information Glut* (London: Abacus, 1997), p. 11.
6 Ibid., pp. 124–5.
7 Ibid., p. 179.
8 Ibid., p. 186.
9 Ibid., p. 191.
10 In Mark Stefik (ed.), *Internet Dreams: Archetypes, Myths, and Metaphors* (Cambridge Massachusetts.: The MIT Press, 1997), p. 209.
11 Shenk, op. cit., p. 213.
12 Harry Edward Neal, *Communications: From Stone Age to Space Age* (London: Phoenix House Ltd., 1960), p. 51.
13 Peter M. Lewis and Corinne Pearlman, *Media and Power* (London: Camden Press, 1986), p. 12.
14 Neal, op.cit., p. 83.
15 Quoted in ibid., p. 98.
16 Ibid., p. 106.
17 Ibid., pp. 109–21.
18 Ibid., pp. 121–4.
19 Ibid., pp. 126–7.
20 Ibid., pp. 128–30.
21 Ibid., pp. 131–2.
22 Joseph N. Pelton, in Mark Long, *World Satellite Almanac* (2nd ed., Indianaopolis: Howard W. Sams & Co., 1987), p. xvi.

23 Long, op. cit., p. 3.
24 Marshall McLuhan, *Understanding Media* (London: Routledge & Kegan Paul Ltd., 1987), pp. 7ff.
25 Philip Marchand, *Marshall McLuhan: The Medium and The Message* (New York: Ticknor & Fields, 1989), pp. 49, 69, 145.
26 Ibid., pp. 121, 130–1.
27 Ibid., p. 231.
28 Robert Thompson, *Defeating Communist Insurgency* (London: Chatto & Windus, 1966), p. 28.
29 John Cloake, *Templer: Tiger of Malaya* (London: Harrap, 1985), p. 262.
30 Thompson, op.cit., p. 16.
31 J. M. Roberts, *The Pelican History of the World*, (Rev. Ed., London: Penguin Group, 1980), p. 972.

CHAPTER II THE PRAGMATIC FIXATION

1 *The Times* (London), 28 January 1998, p. 1.
2 *The Concise Encyclopedia of Western Philosophers and Philosophy* (London: Hutchinson, 1975), p. 232.
3 Ibid., p. 233.
4 Morton White, *Pragmatism and the American Mind* (New York: Oxford University Press, 1975), p. 95.
5 Daniel Bell, *The End of Ideology* (New York: The Free Press, 1962; London: Collier-Macmillan, 1962).
6 Bell, op. cit., pp. 393, 400–3.
7 Daniel Bell, *The Coming of Post-Industrial Society* (London: Heinemann Educational Books, 1974), pp. 126–7, 487–8.
8 Alvin Toffler, *Future Shock* (New York: Bantam Books, 1970).
9 Alvin Toffler, *The Third Wave* (London: William Collins Sons & Co. Ltd., 1980).
10 Charles A. Reich, *The Greening of America* (New York: Random House, 1970).
11 Ibid., p. 4.
12 Ibid., pp. 25, 67.
13 Ibid., pp. 225–6.
14 Ibid., pp. 234 *ff.*
15 Ibid., p. 352.
16 Ibid., pp. 394–5.
17 Arnold J. Wolf, "Consciousness Focus," *Yale Alumni Magazine*, November, 1974, p. 21.
18 Francis Fukuyama, *The End of History and The Last Man* (London: Penguin Books Ltd., 1992).
19 Zbigniew Brzezinski, *The Grand Failure: The Birth and Death of Communism in the Twentieth Century.* (New York: Scribner, 1985).

20 Fukuyama, op. cit., p. xi.

21 Idem.

22 Ibid., pp. 45–6.

23 Mohammed Reza Shah Pahlavi, *Mission for My Country* (New York: McGraw-Hill Book Company, Inc., 1962).

24 Ibid., p. 47.

25 D. R. Denman, *The King's Vista* (Berkhamsted, Herts., UK: Geographical Publications Limited, 1973).

26 Quoted in Donald Wilhelm, *Emerging Indonesia* (2nd ed., London: Quiller Press Limited, 1985, pp. 167–8).

27 Martin Goldsmith and Rosemary Harley, *Who Is My Neighbour?: World Faith and Christian Witness* (London: Scripture, 1988), p. 58.

28 Chris Harrie and Peter Chippendale, *What Is Islam?* (London: W. H. Allen, 1990), p. 3.

29 Norman Davies, *Europe: A History* (London: Pimlico, 1997), p. 641.

30 Harrie and Chippendale, op. cit., p. 234. *Cf.* also John L. Exposito, *The Islamic Threat: Myth or Reality?* (New York: Oxford University Press, 1992).

31 *The Koran: A Translation by N. J. Dawood* (London: Allen Lane, 1967), pp. 22, 31, 128, 190, 196, 253, 281.

32 Goldsmith and Harley, op. cit., idem.

33 Bernard Lewis, *The Arabs in History* (London: Hutchinson, 1985), p. 133.

34 Brian Easlea, *Liberation and the Aims of Science: An Essay on Obstacles to the Building of a Beautiful World* (London: Chatto & Windus, 1973), p. 167.

CHAPTER III GIANTS OF SCIENCE

1 Anita Phillips, *A Defence of Masochism* (London: Faber and Faber Ltd., 1998), p. 45.

2 Donald Wilhelm, *Writing for Profit* (New York: McGraw-Hill Book Company, Inc., 1942), p. vii.

3 Michael White, *Isaac Newton: The Last Sorcerer* (London: Fourth Estate Limited, 1997), p. 4.

4 Quoted in G. M. Trevelyan, *Trinity College: A History and Guide* (Cambridge: Cambridge University Press, 1962), p. 7. New evidence, as reported in *The Sunday Times* (London), 11 October 1998, p. 1.4, has indicated that scientists have confirmed that after more than 350 years the original Newton apple tree is still alive at Woolsthorpe Manor, having been able to re-root and rejuvenate itself. *Cf.* also E. N. da C. Andrade, *Sir Isaac Newton* (New York: Doubleday, 1958); H. D. Anthony, *Sir Isaac Newton* (New York: Abelard-Shuman, 1960);

128 *The Fourth Way*

Arthur E. Bell, *Newtonian Science* (London: Edward Arnold, 1961); H. McLacklan, *Sir Isaac Newton: Theological Manuscripts* (Liverpool: Liverpool University Press, 1950).

5 Anthony, op. cit., p. 150.

6 McLacklan, op. cit., pp. 1, 2.

7 Anthony, op. cit., p. 197.

8 White, op. cit., pp. 395–99.

9 Humphrey Davy, *Salmonia; or Days of Fly Fishing* (4th Ed; London: John Murray, 1851).

10 Thomas Edward Thorpe, *Humphrey Davy: Poet and Philosopher* (London: Cassell, 1896. *Cf.* also Humphrey Davy, *Collected Works* (London: Smith Elder, 1839–40; Joshua Cravan Gregory, *The Scientific Achievements of Sir H. Davy* (London: Humphrey Milford, 1930); James Kendall, *Humphrey Davy* (London: Faber and Faber Ltd., 1959); Humphrey Davy, *Elements of Agricultural Chemistry:* (2nd Ed., London: Longman, Hurst, Rees, Orme, and Brown, 1814); Humphrey Davy, *On the Safety Lamp* (London: R. Hunter, 1815).

11 John Meurig Thomas, *Michael Faraday and the Royal Institution* (Bristol and Philadelphia: Institute of Physics Publishing, 1991). *Cf.* also J. Gordon Cook, *Michael Faraday* (London: Adam & Charles Black, 1963); Michael Faraday, *A Course of Six Lectures on the Chemical History of a Candle* (New York, Crowell, 1957); James Kendall, *Michael Faraday* (London: Faber and Faber, 1957); Charles P. May, *Michael Faraday and the Electric Dynamo* (London: Chatto & Windus, 1961).

12 Patrice Debre, *Louis Pasteur* (Baltimore & London: The Johns Hopkins University Press, 1998), review commentary by Anthony Daniels, *The Sunday Telegraph* (London), The Sunday Review, 18 October 1998, p. 15. *Cf.* also Hilaire Cuny, *Louis Pasteur: The Man and His Theories* (New York: Hill & Wang, 1965); Rene Dubos, *Pasteur and Modern Science* (New York: Doubleday, 1960); Gerald L. Geison, *The Private Science of Louis Pasteur* (Princeton: Princeton University Press, 1995); Madeleine P. Grant, *Louis Pasteur* (New York: McGraw-Hill, 1959); Jacques Nicolle, *Louis Pasteur: A Master of Scientific Inquiry* (London: Scientific Book Guild, 1962).

CHAPTER IV THE GREAT EXPERIMENT

1 Orlando Figes, *A People's Tragedy: The Russian Revolution, 1891–1924* (London: Pimlico, 1997); Robert Service, *A History of Twentieth-Century Russia* (London: Allen Lane, The Penguin Press, 1997); Gregory L. Freeze, Ed, *Russia: A History* (Oxford: Oxford University Press, 1997).

2 P. N. Fedoseyev *et. al.*, *Karl Marx: A Biography* (Moscow: Progress Publishers, 1973), p. 9.

3 Idem.

4 Terry Eagleton, *Marx and Freedom* (London: Phoenix, 1997), p. 3.

5 *Hutchinson's New 20th Century Encyclopedia* (London: Hutchinson, 1974), p. 711.

6 *International Encyclopedia of the Social Sciences* (New York: The Macmillan Company & The Free Press, 1968), vol. 10, pp. 40–1.

7 Karl Marx and Friedrich Engels, *The Communist Manifesto* (Hamondsworth, Middlesex: Penguin Books, 1975), p. 85.

8 Ibid., p. 121.

9 Edward Jay Epstein, *The Invisible Wars between the KGB and the CIA* (New York: Simon and Schuster, 1968), p. 129.

10 Figes, op. cit., p. xvii.

11 Roland W. Clark, *Lenin: The Man Behind the Mask* (London: Faber and Faber, 1988).

12 Ibid., pp. 301–8.

13 Ibid., pp. 376–7.

14 Idem.

15 Robert Conquest, *Lenin* (London: Fontana/Collins, 1972), pp. 98, 100.

16 Clark, op. cit., p. 415.

17 Conquest, op. cit., p. 107.

18 Epstein, op. cit., pp. 129–31.

19 Ibid., pp. 140–3.

20 Idem.

21 Clark, op. cit., p. 492.

22 Brian Moynahan, *The Russian Century* (London: Pimlico, 1994), p. 110.

23 Figes, op. cit., pp. 159–62.

24 Moynahan, op. cit., pp. 106–7.

25 Figes, op. cit., p. 779.

26 Quoted in ibid, p. 780.

27 Quoted in Clark, op. cit., p. 437.

28 Service, op. cit., p. 155.

29 Clark, op. cit., p. 474.

30 Ibid., p. 492.

31 Quoted by R. N. Carew Hunt in *A Guide to Communist Jargon* (London: Coles, 1957), p. 32.

32 Alexander Solzhenitsyn, *The Gulag Archipelago: 1918–1956* (London: Collins & Harvill Press, 1975). *Cf.* also Janusy Bardach and Kathleen Gleeson, *Man Is Wolf to Man: Surviving Stalin's Gulag* (London: Simon and Schuster, 1998).

33 Alexander Solzhenitsyn (Ed.) *From Under the Rubble* (London: Collins & Harvill Press, 1975).

34 Andrei D. Sakharov, *Sakharov Speaks* (London: Collins & Harvill Press, 1974).
35 Andrei D. Sakharov, *My Country and the World* (London: Collins & Harvill Press, 1975), pp. 12–13.
36 Mikhail Gorbachev, *Perestroika: New Thinking for Our Country and the World* (London: William Collins & Co. Ltd., 1987).
37 Ibid., pp. 18–29, 23–4, 66, 11, 156.
38 Ibid., pp. 36–7.
39 Ibid., p. 86.
40 Service, op. cit., pp. 465, 487.
41 *Cf. The Economist* (London), 12 December 1998, pp. 45–6.
42 Conquest, op. cit., pp. 98–100.

CHAPTER V SCIENTIFIC IDEALISM

1 Karl Marx, *Capital: A Critical Analysis of Capitalist Production*, (Moscow: Progress Publishers, 1974), Vol I, p. 173.
2 *Marxism, Communism and Western Society: A Comparative Encyclopedia* (New York: Herder and Herder, 1973), Vol. VII, pp. 36–7.
3 Marx, *Capital*, op. cit., Vol II, pp. 36–7.
4 Marx, *The Poverty of Philosophy*, (Moscow: Progress Publishers, 1973), p. 95.
5 C. R. Fay, *Palace of Industry, 1851: A Study of the Great Exhibition and its Fruits* (Cambridge, England: Cambridge University Press, 1951).
6 Marx, *A Contribution to the Critique of Political Economy* (London: Lawrence & Wishart, 1979), pp. 20–1.
7 David Kunzle, *Fashion and Fetishism* (Totowa, New Jersey: Rowmond and Littlefield, 1982), pp. 2*ff.*
8 Marianne Thesander, *The Feminine Ideal* (London: Reaktion Books Ltd., 1997).
9 *The Times* (London), 8 January 1999, p. 6.
10 G. C. Field, *The Philosophy of Plato*. (London and New York: Oxford University Press, 1961).
11 Werner Heisenberg, *Physics and Philosophy: The Revolution in Modern Science* (London: Allen & Unwin, 1958), pp. 168–9.
12 David Berman, *George Berkeley: Idealism and the Man* (Oxford: Clarendon Press, 1996), pp. 1–2.
13 Quoted in Mary W. Calkins (ed.), *Berkeley Selections* (New York: Scribner, 1929), p. 142.
14 Virgilius Ferm, *A History of Philosophical Systems* (New York: Philosophical Library, 1960), Ch. XXV.
15 A. J. Ayer, *The Revolution in Philosophy* (London: Macmillan, 1963), p. 86.

16 David Dietz, *Atomic Science, Bombs and Power* (New York: Collier Books, 1961).

17 Carl R. Theiler, *Men and Molecules* (London: Harrap, 1960; New York: Dodd, Mead, 1962), p. 201.

18 Cavendish Museum, *Selected Apparatus in the Cavendish Museum.* (Cambridge, England: Cambridge University Press, 1998), pp. 8–9.

19 Richard P. Feynman, *The Meaning of It All.* (London: Allen Lane, 1998), p. 36.

20 C. P. Snow, *The Two Cultures: and a Second Look* (Cambridge and New York: Cambridge University Press, 1964), p. 60.

21 C. R. Leslie, *Memoirs of the Life of John Constable* (London: Phaidon Press; New York: Graphic Press, 1951), pp. 293 *ff.*

22 Kurt Badt, *John Constable's Clouds.* (London: Routledge & Kegan Paul, 1950).

23 Leslie, op. cit.

24 Robert C. Solomon and Kathleen M. Higgins, *A Short History of Philosophy* (New York: Oxford University Press, 1996), p. 303.

25 Timothy Bewes, *Cynicism and Postmodernity.* (London: Verso, 1997), p. 26.

26 Alan Bullock, Oliver Stallybrass and Stephen Trombley, (eds.), *The Fontana Dictionary of Modern Thought* (2nd Ed., London: Fontana Press, 1977), pp. 671–2.

27 Fredric Jameson *The Cultural Turn* (London: Verso, 1998). *Cf.* also Fredric Jameson and Masso Miyosi (eds.), *The Cultures of Globalization* (Durham, N.C. and London: Duke University Press, 1998).

CHAPTER VI THE GLOBAL SYNTHESIS

1 Anthony Giddens, *The Third Way: The Renewal of Social Democracy,* (Cambridge, England: Polity Press, 1998).

2 *The Economist* (London), 19 September 1998, p. 48.

3 Tony Blair, *New Britain: My Vision of a Young Country,* (London: Fourth Estate, 1996).

4 Adapted from Giddens, op. cit, p. 155.

5 Idem.

6 *The Economist,* 19 September, 1998, idem.

7 Tony Blair, *The Third Way: New Politics for the New Century* (London: Fabian Society, 1999), p. 2.

8 James Bryant Conant, *On Understanding Science: An Historical Approach* (New Haven: Yale University Press, 1947), p. xiii (italics added).

9 Ibid., p. 49 (italics added).

10 *The Times* (London), 5 September 1927, p. 15.

11 H. R. H. Prince Philip, The Duke of Edinburgh, "The Impact of

Science on the Human Community," *The Advancement of Science* (London: November, 1963), p. 188.

12 Quoted by Ivor Jennings, in *The Queen's Government* (Harmondsworth, Middlesex: Penguin Books, 1954), p. 9.

13 Printed in William Miller (ed.), *Readings in American Values* (Englewood Cliffs, NJ: Prentice-Hall, Inc., 1964), p. 55.

14 Ibid., pp. 85–6.

15 Ibid., p. 296.

16 Ibid., p. 342.

17 *Universal Declaration of Human Rights: Final Authorized Text* (New York: United Nations Office of Information, 1972), pp. 3–6.

18 Robert Burchfield, *The English Language* (Oxford: Oxford University Press, 1986), p. 2.

19 *The Holy Bible: Revised Standard Edition.* (Oxford: Oxford University Press, 1952), p. 10.

20 Simon Potter, *Our English Language* (London: Penguin Books Ltd., 1987), p. 175.

21 Robert McCrum, William Cran and Robert MacNeil, *The Story of English* (London: Faber & Faber, 1988), pp. 19–20.

22 Ibid., pp. 38–9.

23 Burchfield, op. cit., p. 169.

24 Crum *et al.*, op. cit., pp. 42–3.

25 Quoted in ibid., pp. 32–3.

26 Michael White, op. cit., pp. 1, 3, 340–7.

27 John Maynard Keynes, *The Economic Consequences of the Peace* (New York: Harcourt, Brace and Howe, 1920).

28 Quoted in Rupert Christiansen (ed.), *Cambridge Arts Theatre: Celebrating Sixty Years* (Cambridge, England: Granta Editions, 1996), p. 10.

29 John Kenneth Galbraith, "*How Keynes Came to America,*" in Milo Keynes (ed.), *Essays on John Maynard Keynes* (Cambridge, England: Cambridge University Press).

30 John Kenneth Galbraith, *A History of Economics: The Past as the Present,* (London: Penguin Books, 1987), pp. 222–7.

31 Robert Skidelsky, *Keynes* (Oxford: Oxford University Press, 1996), pp. 11, 77.

32 Galbraith, *A History of Economics,* op. cit., p. 127.

33 Skidelsky, op. cit., p. 89. See also Robert Skidelsky, *John Maynard Keynes,* Vol.2, *The Economist As Saviour* (London: MacMillan London Limited, 1992).

34 Paul A. Samuelson and William D. Nordhaus, *Economics* (Sixteenth Edition, Boston: Irwin McGraw-Hill, 1998), p. 5.

35 D. A. Moggridge, *Keynes* (London: The Macmillan Press Ltd., 1993), p. 13.

36 Donald Wilhelm, *Emerging Indonesia* (London: Cassell, 1980); New and Enlarged Edition, London: Quiller Press, 1985).

37 *Financial Times* (London), 4 January 1999, p. 20.

38 *Financial Times* (London), 6/7 March 1999, p. 2.

39 Robert L. Chapman (ed.). *The Macmillan Dictionary of American Slang* (London: Macmillan Press, 1995).

40 Roger Scruton, *An Intelligent Person's Guide to Modern Culture* (London: Duckworth, 1998), pp. 89–90.

41 Geraldine Norman, *The Hermitage: The Biography of a Great Museum* (London: Pimlico, 1999).

Index

Academy of Medicine, 53
accelerators, particle, 88–9
action, 59
Adam, Robert, 3
aid, 66–7, 117–19
air-mail, 8
Alexander the Great, 121
alienation, 23
alloys, 38
American Relief Administration
    (ARA), 66–7
Amnesty International, 108
anthrax, 55–6
antiseptic system, 54–5
apple, fall of from a tree, 36
armed forces, purge of, 64
art, 35, 94–6
Ashby, Lord, 104
Asian meltdown, 75, 116
atomic nucleus, 88–9
atomic weapons, 71, 86, 101–2
autoclave, 53

Babel, 109
Baird, John Logie, 11
Barlard, Professor, 49
beet sugar, 52
Bell, Alexander Graham, 9
Bell, Daniel, 20–1

Bell Telephone Laboratories,
    11
benzene, 45–6
Berkeley, George, 83–5, 93
Berlin Wall, 70
Bewes, Timothy, 96
Bible, 108–9
bilateral aid programmes, 118
Bill of Rights, 105
biology, 48–56
Bishop of Ripon, 103
Black Monday 1929, 113
Blair, Tony, xiii, xiv, 99, 100–1
Bohr, Niels, 87
Boswell, James, 84
Bourdon (painter), 95
bourgeoisie, 60
Britain, 115
    Malayan Emergency, 15–16
British Broadcasting Corporation
    (BBC), 11, 108
    World Service, 109
British Executive Service
    Overseas, 118
Brzezinski, Zbigniew, 24
bubble chamber, 92
bubbles, soap, 39
Burchfield, Robert, 108, 111
Burma, 107–8

Burns, Robert, 3

calculus, 38
Cambridge Arts Theatre, 112
Cambridge University, 35–6, 104,
    111
cancellation of external debt, 117
Caxton, William, 7
Chappe, Claude, 7
Cheka, 62–3, 65
chemistry
    Davy, 39–43
    Pasteur, 48–56
chiaroscuro, 95
chicken cholera, 55
Chippendale, P., 31
chlorine, 42, 45
cholera, chicken, 55
Christianity, 31, 33, 116
Churchill, Winston S., 68, 111
Clark, Roland, W., 62, 65
Clark, Arthur C., 12
class, 60
Clinton, Bill, xiii, xiv, 18, 99
Clinton, Hillary, xiii, 18, 99
cloud chamber, 91–2
clouds, 94–5
CNN, 108
Cockcroft, John, 88
Coleridge, Samuel Taylor, 40, 96
collectivization 65–6, 68, 69
colour television, 11
communications, evolution of,
    5–14
Communism, 13, 25–6, 119
    history of Soviet Russia under,
        58–77
    Iranian response to, 28–9
    Malayan Emergency and
        Vietnam War, 15–17
Communist Manifesto, The, 59–60
Conant, James Bryant, 101–2
Conquest, Robert, 62, 76

consciousness, 21, 80
    Consciousness I, II and III,
        22–4
Constable, John, 94–6
constants of nature, 101–4
corruption, 75, 116, 117
corsets, 81–2
couriers, 7, 8
Cran, William, 110
crystals, 50, 51
Cuban missile crisis, 70
cultural revolt, 101, 119–21, 122
cultural side-effects of economic
        growth, 29–30

Daniels, Anthony, 56
data smog, 4–5
Davy, Sir Humphrey, 39–44, 48,
    96
Debre, Patrice, 56
debt, international, 117
Declaration of Independence,
    104
deficit financing, 113, 114–15
DeForest, Lee, 10
democratic consensus, 24–6
developing countries, 117–18
development, 16, 27–8, 29–30,
    76
Dewey, John, 19
diamonds, 43
differential calculus, 38
Diocletian, Emperor, 8
Disinformation Service, 61, 63–4
dissidents, 70–2
dynamo, 46–7

Eagleton, Terry, 59
Easlea, Brian, 33
economic development, 16, 27–8,
    29–30, 76
economic reform, 75–6
Edinburgh, 2–3

education, 27, 30
Egyptians, 6
Einstein, Albert, 85–6
electric motor, 45
electricity
    Davy and, 41–2
    Faraday, 44–8
electrolysis, 41, 42, 47
electromagnetic energy, 87
electromagnetic induction, 46
electronic servitude, 5
electrostatic machine, 44
elements, chemical, 42
Encyclopaedia Britannica, 3, 44
enemies of the people, 65
energy, mass and, 85–6, 88
Engels, Friedrich, 60
English language, 7
    role of, 101, 108–11, 122
English-Speaking Union, 111
environment, natural, 20
epistemology, 82–90
Epstein, Edward Jay, 61
extermination camps, Nazi, 71
external debt, 117
Extraordinary Commission for
        Combatting
    Counter-Revolution,
        Speculation and Sabotage
        (Cheka), 62–3, 65

famine, 65–7
Faraday, Michael, 43–8
female fashion, 82
fermentation, 52
Feynman, Richard P., 93
Figes, Orlando, 58, 61–2, 67
Fillmore, Laura, 5
financial aid, 117
firedamp (methane), 43
Fisher, David, 64
Food and Agriculture
    Organization, 118

Four Freedoms declaration,
    105–6
free-market economy, 75–6
Freeze, Gregory L., 58
French Academy of Sciences, 53
Fukuyama, Francis, 24–6

Galbraith, John Kenneth, 113, 114
Gates, Bill, 1
Gay-Lussac, Joseph Louis, 49–50
germ theory, 51–6, 102
Germany, 112
    role in Marxism-Leninism, 61,
        63–4
Giddens, Anthony, xiii, 99–100
Glaser, D.A., 92
glasnost (openness), 73
global problems, 1–2
Gorbachev, Mikhail, 72–5, 76
Gorky, Maxim, 67
grain, requisitioning of, 65–6
gravitation, 36
Great Depression, 113–14, 115
Great Exhibition 1851, 80
Gutenberg, Johann, 7

Harrie, C., 31
Hegel, Georg Wilhelm Friedrich,
    85
Heisenberg, Werner, 83
Henry, Joseph, 46
Hermitage, 120
Herodotus, 8
Higgins, Kathleen M., 96
Hitler, Adolf, 64, 112, 113
Hoover, Herbert, 66, 113–14
human rights, 71, 122
    benchmarks, 101, 104–8
Hume, David, 3
Hungary, 70
hydrochloric acid, 42

Ibadan, University of, 116

ideal: and reality, 95
ideology
    end of, 20–1
    ideological assistance, 119
    initiative in Malayan
        Emergency, 16
    intellectual system of Fourth
        Way, 101–21, 122–3
    vacuum in Soviet Union and
        Russia, 70–6
Ife, University of, 116
immaterialism, 84–5
immunization, 55–6
Indonesia, 116
industrialization, 76
information overload, 4–5
information technology (IT), 1,
    4
Institute for Public and Business
    Administration, 26–7
instrumentation, 90–3
integral calculus, 38
intellectual interaction, 124
intellectual trends, 20–6
intellectuals, new, 3–4
Intermediate Technology
    Development Group
    (ITDG), 118
International Bank for
    Reconstruction and
    Development (IBRD),
    117
International Monetary Fund
    (IMF), 117
International Executive Service
    Corps, 118
international mixed economy,
    101, 116–19, 122
Internet, 4, 5, 108
iodine, 43
Iran, 26–31, 121
Iranian Revolution, 28–31
Iraq, 31

Islam, 26, 31–2, 116
    Iran, 27, 28, 29, 30–1

James, William, 19
Jameson, Fredric, 97
Japan, 107, 116
Jeans, Sir James, 87
Jefferson, Thomas, 104
Jenner, Edward, 55
John, King, 104
Johnson, Samuel, 84

Kant, Immanuel, 85
KDKA, 10–11
Keynes, John Maynard, 102,
    111–16, 122
Keynes, John Neville, 112, 115
Keynesian legacy, 101, 111–16,
    122
Khomeini, Ayatollah, 29
Khrushchev, Nikita S., 69–70,
    119
Kirov ballet company, 120
Koran, The, 32
kulaks, 65, 68, 69
Kunzle, David, 81, 82

labour camps, 64, 65, 71
lactic acid, 52
land reforms, 27–8
language, 6
    English *see* English language
Lawrence, Ernest O., 88
Leibniz, Gottfried Wilhelm, 38
Lenin, V.I., 61–9, 74
Lenin Museum, 25
Leningrad *see* St Petersburg
Lewis, Bernard, 32
liberal democracy, 24–6
light, 37, 47
lighthouses, 48
liquefied gases, 45
Lister, Joseph, 54–5

Literacy Corps, 27, 30
livestock, slaughter of, 66
Long, Mark, 12–13
Lopokova, Lydia, 112
low-intensity warfare, 15–16

MacNeil, Robert, 110
macroeconomics, 115
magnetic lines of force, 47
magnetism, 44–5, 46–7
mail-coach, 8
Malayan Emergency, 15–16
Manhattan Project, 101–2
Marchand, Philip, 13–14
Marconi, Guglielmo, 9–10,
    11
Marx, Karl Heinrich, 58–60,
    78–80
Marx Memorial Library, 78
Marxism-Leninism *see*
    Communism
masochism
  emotional/spiritual, 35
  sublimated, 81–2
mass, energy and, 85–6, 88
materialistic science, 83, 93–4
McLuhan, Marshall, 13–14
McCrum, Robert, 110
media: nature and content of
    message, 13–14
mixed economy, international,
    101, 116–19, 122
modernization, 16, 27–8, 29–30,
    76
Moggridge, D.E., 115
Morse, Samuel F.B., 8–9
motor, electric, 45
movable type, 7
Moynahan, Brian, 65–6
multidisciplinary man, 3–4
multidisciplinary scientists, 35–57
multidisciplinary strategic vision,
    15–17

music, 23

National Bureau of Standards,
    114
NATO, 108
natural science *see* science
nature, 21, 78–9, 95–6
  constants of, 101–4
Nazi extermination camps, 71
Neal, Harry E., 6, 7
Nepmen, 68
New Economic Policy (NEP), 68,
    69
New Labour, 100
Newton, Isaac, 35–9, 81, 93, 112,
    122
Nigeria, 116
nitrous oxide, 41
non-material elements, 23–4
Nordhaus, William D., 115
Noyce, Robert, 97
Nu, U., 107
nuclear weapons, 71, 86, 101–2
nucleus, atomic, 88–9

observation, 90–1
Oersted, Hans Christian, 44–5
oil prices, 29
OKW (German High Command),
    61
'Operation Kama', 63–4
optical deception, 47–8
Ottoman Empire, 31

Pahlavi, Mohammed Reza Shah,
    27–30
Pahlavi, Reza Shah, 27
papyrus, 6
Paris Peace Conference, 112
Parsons, Sir Anthony, 28
partial heat sterilisation
    (pasteurization), 53–4
particle accelerators, 88–9

particles, subatomic, 47, 88–9, 91–2
Pasteur, Louis, 48–56, 96, 102, 123
Peace Corps, 118
peaceful coexistence, 69–70
Peirce, C.S., 18–19
perestroika (restructuring), 72–3, 74
Peter the Great, 76, 121
Pharamaceutical Society of Paris, 50–1
Philip, Prince (Duke of Edinburgh), 103
Phillips, Anita, 35
philosophical idealism, 82–5
Plato, 82
Pneumatics Institution, 40–1
polarimeter, 50, 51
Porlase, Mr, 40
post-industrial society, 21–2
post-modernism, 96–7
post-pragmatic intellectual, 20, 33–4
postal services, 8
potassium, 42
Potter, Simeon, 110
practice, theory and, 37–9, 86
pragmatic syndrome, 14, 18–34
pragmatism, 18–20
Preece, Sir William, 10
printing, 7
prism, glass, 37
privatization, 75
productive forces, 60, 78–80
public expenditure, 114
public-spirited Russians, 66
purge of armed forces, 64

quantum theory, 87–9

rabies vaccine, 56
racemic acid, 49–50, 50–1

radio, 9–11
Radio Moscow, 109
Raeburn, Henry, 3
railway industry, 8
Read, Anthony, 64
reality, 14, 21, 22–3, 82
ideal and, 95–6
reason, 22–3
Red Terror, 62–3
reflecting telescope, 37–8
Reich, Charles A., 22–4
religion, 39, 93–4
Rembrandt van Rijn, 95
reproduction, 53
rockets, 12
Romans, 6
Roosevelt, Franklin D., 86, 105–6, 114
Roosevelt, Theodore, 105
Rossiter, Clinton, 58
Royal Institution, 41–2
Royal Meteorological Society, 95
Rumford, Count, 41
Russia, 116–17, 124
ideological and technical assistance programme, 119
Marxist experiment, 58–77
see also St Petersburg
Russian Revolution, 61–2

safety lamp, 43
St Petersburg, Russia, 25, 76, 120–1, 124
siege of Leningrad, 69, 121
Sakharov, Andrei D., 70, 71–2, 108
Samuelson, Paul A., 115
satellites, 11–13
science, 33
materialistic, 83, 93–4
multidisciplinary scientists, 35–57

social application of, 101–4,
    122
scientific idealism, 56, 78–98, 123
scientific socialism, 58–77
Scott, Sir Walter, 3
Scruton, Roger, 119–20
secular-spiritual distinction, 31–3
seed, 67
self, 23
semaphore, 7
Service, Robert, 58, 68, 74
Sharia (Islamic law), 32
Shenk, David, 4–5
Shia Islam, 30–1
show trials, 63
silk industry, 54
Skidelsky, Robert, 113, 115
Smith, Adam, 3
Smith, Sydney, 2
Snow, C.P., 93–4
soap bubbles, 39
social application of science,
    101–4, 122
social science, 33
social world, 21
socialism *see* Communism
Society for International
    Development, 118
Soloman, Robert C., 96
Solzhenitsyn, Alexander, 70–1,
    108
Soros, George, 117
Soviet Union, 17, 29, 100
    Marxist-Leninist experiment,
        61–74
    technological and ideological
        assistance programme, 119
specialists, 1–2
spectrum, visible, 37
spiritual-secular distinction, 31–3
spores, 53
Sputnik I, 11–12, 13
stagnation, 70, 72, 73

stainless steels, 45
Stalin, Joseph, 63, 64–5, 68–9
Stephenson, George, 8
Stodart (Faraday's collaborator),
    45
Stukeley, William, 36
Sturgeon, William, 46
subatomic particles, 47, 88–9,
    91–2
submarine telegraphy, 9
sugar beet, 52
Sunni Islam, 30
superior theories, 102

tartaric acid, 49–50, 51
technical assistance, 118, 119
technics, 21
technology, 20, 23–4, 80
    media, 13–14
    and philosophical idealism, 83
Tehran, University of, 26–7
telegraphy, 8–9
telephone, 9
telescope, reflecting, 37–8
television, 4–5, 11
Templer, General (later Field
    Marshal) Sir Gerald, 15–16
terror, 62–3
theory, and practice, 37–9, 86
Thesander, Marianne, 81
Third Way, xiii, xiv, 99–101
Thomas, John Meurig, 43
Thompson, Sir Robert, 15
tight-laced corsets, 81–2
Toffler, Alvin, 21–2
transistor, 11, 12
Trinity House, 48
type, movable, 7

unemployment relief projects,
    114
United Nations (UN), 106, 108,
    118

United Nations Industrial Development Organization, 118
United States, 19, 29
  Great Depression, 113–14
  greening of America, 22–3
  human rights, 104–6
  Keynesian economic policy, 114–15
  Vietnam War, 14–15, 16–17
Universal Declaration of Human Rights, 106–7
Urmson, J.O., 19

V2, 12
vaccination, 55–6
value-free analysis, 33
valve, 10
Van de Graaff, Robert J., 88
Versailles Treaty, 64
Victoria, Queen, 9
Vienna, 31
Vietnam War, 14–15, 16–17
vision, 15–17
Voice of America, 109
Voltaic pile, 41
Voluntary Service Overseas, 118

Walton, E.T.S., 88
Watson, Thomas A., 9

Watt, Gregory, 40
Watt, James, 40
wax-coated wood, 6
Western advice to Russia, 76–7
Western economic and cultural values, 29–30
White, Michael, 35–6
White, Morton, 19
Wilhelm, Donald (father), 35, 66–7
Wilson, C.T.R., 91–2, 96
Win, Ne, 107–8
Wolf, Arnold J., 24
women, 81–2
Woolsthorpe Manor, 36
Wordsworth, William, 36, 96
working class, 60
World Health Organization, 118
World War I, 61
World War II, 69
Wright Brothers, 102–3
writers, 35
writing surfaces, 6

Yeltsin, Boris, 75–6
Yemen, 119
Young, Douglas, 3
youth, 119–20
Yugoslavia, 108